P9-DDW-918

# Teaching Phonics Today
## A Primer for Educators

Dorothy S. Strickland
Rutgers, the State University of New Jersey
New Brunswick, New Jersey, USA

INTERNATIONAL
Reading
Association

800 Barksdale Road, PO Box 8139
Newark, Delaware 19714-8139, USA
www.reading.org

The International Reading Association attempts, through its publications, to provide a forum for a wide spectrum of opinions on reading. This policy permits divergent viewpoints without implying the endorsement of the Association.

**Director of Publications**   Joan M. Irwin
**Assistant Director of Publications**   Wendy Lapham Russ
**Managing Editor, Books
   and Electronic Publications**   Christian A. Kempers
**Associate Editor**   Matthew W. Baker
**Assistant Editor**   Janet S. Parrack
**Assistant Editor**   Mara P. Gorman
**Publications Coordinator**   Beth Doughty
**Association Editor**   David K. Roberts
**Production Department Manager**   Iona Sauscermen
**Graphic Design Coordinator**   Boni Nash
**Electronic Publishing Supervisor**   Wendy A. Mazur
**Electronic Publishing Specialist**   Anette Schütz–Ruff
**Electronic Publishing Specialist**   Cheryl J. Strum
**Electronic Publishing Assistant**   Peggy Mason

**Photo Credits**   Dorothy Strickland, pp. 35, 49, 83; Nancy Alexander, p. 54.

**Library of Congress Cataloging in Publication Data**
Strickland, Dorothy S.
   Teaching phonics today: A primer for educators / Dorothy S. Strickland
      p.   cm.
   Includes bibliographical references and index.
   1. Reading–Phonetic method.   I. Title.
LB1573.3.S77   1998                                           97–43795
372.46'5–dc21
ISBN 0–87207–184–7
Fourth Printing, March 1999

# Contents

**INTRODUCTION**                                                              1

**CHAPTER 1**   What Is Phonics and Why Is It                                 4
                Such a Controversial Topic?

**CHAPTER 2**   How Readers and Writers                                       14
                Use Phonics

**CHAPTER 3**   How Have Changes in Literacy                                  26
                Instruction Influenced the Teaching
                of Phonics?

**CHAPTER 4**   Finding the Balance: Systematic,                             48
                Intensive, Code–Driven Phonics
                Versus Holistic, Embedded,
                Meaning–Driven Approaches

**CHAPTER 5**   Learning Phonics: Strategies That                            53
                Support Beginning Readers and Writers

**CHAPTER 6**   Shaping Curriculum:                                          67
                Instruction and Assessment

**CHAPTER 7**   Articulating the Phonics Program                             81
                to Parents and the Community

**APPENDIX**                                                                 90

**REFERENCES**                                                               96

**INDEX**                                                                    101

# Introduction

I can think of no better way to introduce this book than to share the text of a letter that describes the essence of what this book is about. The letter was written by an official of a large U.S. educational organization and describes his visit to Dorothy Fowler's first-grade classroom in Falls Church, Virginia, USA. Like so many parents, teachers, and interested citizens, the writer is concerned about the controversies surrounding beginning reading instruction. He has heard a great deal about reading debates and the need for balanced instruction. A friend of Dorothy's and mine suggested that he visit her classroom to see high-quality instruction first hand. This is precisely what he saw, as is indicated by the following:

> Thank you very much for recommending that I visit Dorothy Fowler's first-grade class. It was fun to look around the room. All of her 18 students had their own basket of books, chosen to match their ability. The bulletin boards offered children word attack strategies. The kids' journals were full of nifty writing.
>
> But the real fun for me was watching Dot teach. For $2\frac{1}{2}$ hours her kids moved without incident from one literary activity to another. Every time kids started getting restless it seemed like she moved them on to a new activity.
>
> She had kids doing independent reading, reading in pairs (shoulder to shoulder), and reading in groups of four. She had them spelling, writing, and writing some more. And while they worked individually or in groups, she was teaching kids individually.
>
> She brought the whole class together to teach a phonics lesson on the *aw* sound in words like *drawing*. There were so many nice touches. Without prompting, you could see kids clapping out the sounds in the words. Dot used stick-ups to cover over the blend she was teaching. And, far from relying on the boring worksheets of days gone by, she had her kids using magic markers, boards, and their own mini-erasers to create their own lists of words that sounded like *draw*. Kids would eagerly hold them up for her to see.

For almost 30 minutes, she read her students two books, one fiction and one nonfiction, and talked with her students about the content of those books. The kids understood a lot. I also marveled at the self-control of the kids, until again I realized it was no mistake.

They sat with their legs crossed and their hands folded in. Their teacher had told them they had to do that so that students could come up to the front of the room without stepping on one another's hands and feet. They started the year practicing their behavior every day, Ms. Fowler told me. I was seeing the fruits of that early labor.

If your goal was to send me to see a first-grade teacher who knows reading instruction, I don't think you could have made a better choice. Thank you again. It was the kind of morning that makes me want to be a first-grade teacher...if only it was as easy as Dot Fowler makes it look.

Dorothy is an outstanding teacher, but I think that she would agree that there are many teachers like her throughout the world. Teachers like Dorothy artfully balance the development of skills and strategies within the framework of a rich language and literature program. They know that all aspects of a child's literacy development are interdependent. The public need not worry that such teachers will mindlessly embrace every revolutionary educational trend. On the contrary, they can take comfort in the fact that these teachers eternally are seeking and reflecting on new information and ideas that help inform their work. By and large, teachers are intelligent, skillful, and deeply caring about what they do. This letter is about Dorothy Fowler, a first-rate teacher, but it is so much more. It is about the art and science of good teaching.

Although this book has its focus on phonics, like Dorothy Fowler it is really about the art and science of good teaching. For it is good teaching that helps make phonics work for children as they learn to read and write. The organizational structure for this book reflects my major goal, that of illuminating the black hole of contention surrounding phonics with information that will help educators make wise instructional decisions. The first two chapters set forth the issues that focus on phonics and the controversy they arouse inevitably. Chapters 3 and 4 explain the ways in which reading instruction, particularly the teaching of phonics, has changed in recent years and why. Chapters 5, 6, and 7 offer suggestions for helping children learn to use phonics as a key component of their overall reading development. These chapters also make suggestions for curriculum development and for articulating the phonics program to parents and the community at large.

It is my hope that this book will be a useful tool for those who wish to make sense of a topic that often divides faculties, parents, and community members. There is no doubt that there are legitimate differences among us and these should be acknowledged and valued. There also is considerable common ground among us and an overwhelming similarity of purpose. I invite readers to use this book as a springboard for reflection and discussion and ultimately as a catalyst for making informed instructional decisions that help children become literate human beings.

DSS

# CHAPTER 1

# What Is Phonics and Why Is It Such a Controversial Topic?

Probably no other aspect of reading instruction is more discussed, more hotly debated, and less understood than phonics and its role in learning to read. The phonics debate has been active for many years. However, today, more than ever before, classroom teachers are apt to be confronted by concerned members of the community who have questions about phonics. Given the amount of public interest in this topic, even teachers and administrators in districts where phonics has not become an issue are likely to reexamine their beginning reading programs.

A discussion of phonics often evokes very different viewpoints, some even more disparate than those shown in Figure 1. Those who view phonics and its underpinnings as the most important and fundamental aspect of reading instruction and see it as the ultimate solution to illiteracy are on one side of the argument. Those for whom phonics is a worrisome topic, conjuring up images of children merely calling out the words and barking at print and ignoring meaning, are on the other side. This book is for the large majority of educators, parents, grandparents, and community members who feel discomfort at either end of this continuum. It speaks to those educators who seek to frame educational policy and establish sound instructional practice that values phonics as an important tool for under-standing and using written language within a balanced, comprehensive program for reading and writing. Figure 2 on page 6 explains where phonics fits into the complex process of leading to read.

## What Is Phonics?

*Phonics* refers to instruction in the sound–letter rela-tionship used in reading and writing. It involves an under-standing of the alphabetic principle (that is, there is a rela-tion between spoken sounds and letters or combinations of letters) on which the English language is based and a knowledge of the sounds associated with a particular letter or combination of letters. For example, the letter *b* at the beginning of the word *back* and the combination of letters *ck* at the end of *back* each represent a single sound.

The ability to learn how sounds map to letters is relat-ed to *phonemic awareness*, or the understanding that speech itself is composed of a series of individual sounds (Juel, Griffith, & Gough, 1986; Yopp, 1992). That is, before a child masters sound–symbol associations, he or she must under-stand that spoken words can be segmented. Children who are phonologically aware are able to discriminate between and manipulate sounds in words and syllables in speech.

---

### Figure 1  Opposing Voices

"Today's teachers *don't* teach phonics. Our language is alphabetic. First, children should be taught the letters of the alphabet and the sounds that go with them and then they will be able to read."

"Today's teachers *do* teach phonics. First, children need to learn that reading is sup-posed to make sense. Phonics should be taught, as needed, within the context of learning to read and write."

## Figure 2  Where Phonics Fits in Literacy Learning and Teaching

- *Literacy* involves the ability to solve problems, think critically and creatively, and communicate effectively.
- *Literacy instruction* includes a planned program for the deliberate teaching of word identification skills and strategies that enable students to write effectively and to read with understanding.
- *Instruction for word identification* offers learners a range of organized and relatively systematic strategies to deal with unfamiliar words.
- *Phonics* is the ability to link written symbol and sound; it is included among the word identification strategies taught and learned in a comprehensive literacy program.
- In every subject area, students apply word identification strategies, including phonics, in varied situations with increasingly difficult materials.

They know when words rhyme or do not rhyme. They can indicate when a series of words begin or end with the same sound, such as *dog, dark,* and *dusty,* or *big, tag,* and *frog.* They also can break down or blend a series of sounds, such as /k/–/a/–/t/ in *cat.* Most important, these children can shift their attention from the content of speech to focus on the form of speech before they return to its meaning. Although the role of phonemic awareness in children's literacy development still is not completely clear, most researchers agree that "training in phonological awareness is both possible and advantageous for children" (Ayers, 1993, p. 153). The development of phonemic awareness is generally stressed during kindergarten and early first grade. Some phonics instruction may begin in kindergarten, but it is generally emphasized during first and second grade.

Questions remain about how much phonemic awareness is necessary to develop ability in decoding and how much is acquired in a reciprocal, mutually supportive relationship with learning to read (Perfetti, Beck, Bell, & Hughes, 1987; Weaver, 1997). Teachers and researchers are learning a great deal about how to help young children become aware that spoken language can be taken apart and how this understanding supports and eases the learning of phonics. Kindergarten teachers always have built on children's affinity for the alliteration and rhyme in nursery rhymes and children's songs. Young children also have the benefit of their participation in the language of popular culture, which is filled with terms such as *boombox* or *backpack* that foster sensitivity to the sounds of language.

*Structural analysis* is a term that often is confused with phonics. It involves a knowledge of the structural changes that differentiate words having common roots: inflectional endings (–s, –ed, –ing), prefixes and suffixes (pre–, un–, –tion, –ment), and root words (pre*paid*, un*paid*, re*paid*). Instruction in structural analysis usually begins in first grade, where teachers help children learn about rules such as adding *s* to form plurals and the formation of compound words such as *raincoat* and *snowman*. It continues through children's schooling as they encounter increasingly complex language structures.

> **W**ith respect to the knowledge that is critical to reading, that which can be developed through phonic instruction represents neither the top nor the bottom, but only a realm in between. (Adams, 1990, pp. 421–422)

Over the years, the term phonics has come to mean much more than the definition presented earlier. In the minds of many educators, phonics and beginning reading are synonymous. Indeed, most teachers of beginning reading include a broad array of skills and activities under the heading of phonics. The teaching of letter recognition, rhyming words, and spelling patterns generally is considered to be part of phonics instruction. Phonics often is referred to as a method or program of teaching reading, but it is really a set of instructional strategies that helps learners connect sounds with written symbols. Nevertheless, any instruction that places an emphasis on the teaching of sound–letter correspondences frequently is termed a *phonics method*.

# The Development of the Phonics Controversy

Historically, those who have denounced poor reading achievement in the United States have turned to phonics as a solution. A brief look at some of the historical perspectives and influences on reading instruction help explain the circumstances and conditions that have brought us to where we are today.

During the colonial period in the United States, an alphabet spelling system dominated the teaching of reading. Instruction was directed toward a single purpose, the reading of religious books by a limited few who were actually taught to read. In the early 1800s, Horace Mann introduced the whole-word method of teaching reading. He stressed memorizing entire words before analyzing letters and letter patterns, and he focused on silent reading and reading for comprehension. The *McGuffey Eclectic Readers* also were introduced around this time. These readers made use of the controlled repetition of words and an organizational scheme in which sentence length and vocabulary were controlled to match the developmental level of students.

During the latter half of the 19th century, a phonetics method was introduced in which children were taught individual sound-letter relations and how to blend them to decipher words. Teachers became dissatisfied with this method because too much attention was placed on word analysis and too little attention was given to comprehension. This approach was temporarily abandoned around 1910 and replaced with the "look-and-say" method. This method also proved unsatisfactory to many teachers. Children were expected to learn every word as a sight word, making progress slow and laborious.

About 1920, the silent reading method emerged as the official approach in many schools. This method urged the total abandonment of all oral methods of instruction and assessment. About this time, widespread administration of standardized tests called the public's attention to the vast individual differences in reading achievement among children. It also inspired teachers to try new instructional methods to better accommodate individual differences. Research during this era gave rise to an extremely popular approach that followed—the basal reading program—which was launched throughout the United States in the early 1930s. The "Dick and Jane" readers (and others like them), as basal programs would come to be known, became the staple of reading instruction methodology in the United States for several decades. Basal reading programs held predominance over other methods until the early 1960s, when teachers became dissatisfied with them as the only form of reading instruction and again returned to phonics. Educators wanted more organized skill-development programs and more attention to reading in the content subjects. Specialized phonics programs were introduced into many schools to augment the basal program. (For a more complete description of the changes in approaches to methods of teaching reading see Lapp and Flood, 1978, pp. 427–494.)

The on-again off-again fascination with phonics has been inspired to some extent by media reports of illiteracy among the military, of international events, and of standardized test results. For example, during both World Wars, the U.S. military charged that too many members could not read well enough to follow military instructions. Such reports received considerable attention in the news and understandable concern among the public. During the 1950s and 1960s, media reports of Sputnick, the Cold War, and the threat of atomic weapons also made literacy a national imperative. Interest in reading instruction soared during this period with laymen and the media criticizing the schools' methods and calling for decisive action. One of the most vocal proponents of phonics was Rudolph Flesch, whose book *Why Johnny Can't Read* (1955) hailed phonics as the cure for what he perceived as widespread and growing illiteracy.

Although many children were not learning to read as well as expected, others were reaching new heights of proficiency in reading. Numerous research studies were conducted to determine why some children, particularly poor and minority children, were not succeeding. During the 1960s, educational researchers engaged in numerous studies comparing various approaches to reading instruction in controlled studies designed to demonstrate superiority. The most famous of these, the Cooperative Research Program in First Grade Reading Instruction (commonly referred to as the "First–Grade Studies") was designed to compare a traditional basal program with various other approaches (Bond & Dykstra, 1967; republished with related commentaries in 1997).

> **D**on't waste time debating whether or not to teach phonics, spelling, grammar, and other "skills" of literacy. Do spend time discussing how to teach them in a way that contributes to the learners' "self improvement." (Strickland, 1994–1995, p. 299)

Unfortunately, no strong conclusion could be drawn from these studies. No one approach was so distinctly better in all situations and respects than the others that it could be considered the one best method to be used exclusively. The publication of *Learning to Read: The Great Debate* (Chall, 1967) brought considerable attention to the phonics debate. Chall examined the existing research literature for evidence related to questions regarding the best way to approach beginning reading. She concluded that "a code emphasis tends to produce better overall reading achievement by the beginning of fourth grade than a meaning emphasis" (p. 137). Chall's conclusions regarding beginning instruction were challenged by many (for example, Rutherford, 1968), raising questions about the validity of the research studies on which she based her conclusions and the arbitrary nature of her classification system into code- and meaning–emphasis categories. Although Chall did not suggest that her findings be used to endorse systematic phonics approaches, her work has been highly influential in support of those who endorse a heavy emphasis on phonics in beginning reading.

Various changes in methodology were initiated during the 1960s and early 1970s in an attempt to solve the reading problem in the United States. Programmed materials were developed to provide better classroom management techniques. The language experience approach, which advocated the use of children's own dictated language as an entre to reading, was promoted as an effective teaching method. Linguistics began to influence the structure of some basal readers. Linguists promoted the teaching of reading through patterned word units such as *Pat sat on a mat.* Materials dealing with multiethnic urban environments were introduced to answer the criticism that basals tended to reflect the values and mores of white middle-class America. Teachers were encouraged to address the needs of diverse readers by personalizing programs to suit individual needs. Researchers, educators, and publishers of reading materials continued to address an ever-expanding set of new and complex challenges, as schools faced an increasingly diverse population and a society in which the schools were called on to take on more and more responsibility. Reports, critical of the public schools, such as *A Nation at Risk* (National Commission on Excellence in Education, 1983) reinforced negative public opinion about the schools. Even when statements included in the reports such as the assertion of a decline in overall student achievement in the United States proved to be contradictory or incorrect, disparagement of the schools and the teaching of reading remained constant (Berliner & Biddle, 1995; Kibby 1993).

During the 1990s, reading systems published by a few major publishing companies continued to dominate the materials and methodology used to teach reading. Although these expanded basals differed in some ways, virtually all had changed in similar ways. One of the most noticeable changes was the inclusion of authentic literature, (such as the text of trade books) in the students' anthologies.

Prior to this time, most of the material at the primary-grade levels and some at the elementary levels was written specifically for inclusion in basal reading systems. This was done to maintain control of vocabulary, sentence length, and other factors believed to contribute to readability. The inclusion of authentic literature with relatively few changes from the original text was a major departure. Another important difference was the expansion of reading programs to include instruction in all the language arts, particularly writing and spelling. Many reading programs were now termed "integrated language arts programs" or "total literacy programs," indicating that a separate program for writing and oral language would no longer be needed.

The move toward integrated approaches to the teaching of the English language arts (listening, speaking, reading, and writing) in the elementary schools was inspired by several new directions in the research and thinking of many influential educators in the United States and other English-speaking countries. Perhaps more than ever before, the work of research in the field of reading was informed by cognitive and developmental psychology, sociology, linguistics, literary theory, and a growing interest in research on writing in the elementary school. The ideas generated from this cross fertilization and collaboration of researchers from various disciplines helped to establish a rationale for treating language as a meaningful whole rather than as a set of discrete subskills.

Integrated, literature-based approaches to reading instruction in which phonics is taught in conjunction with other word identification strategies was among the practical applications. The tension between these newer approaches—though widely varied in application—and approaches based on a phonics emphasis or a particular approach to the teaching of phonics continue to be heard today.

Sometimes the support of phonics is combined with demands for a greater emphasis on spelling and grammar and a return to instructional practices of the past. Discussions surrounding these issues often come to represent much more than the concerns associated with reading instruction. In some districts, the phonics controversy reveals deep philosophical differences about teaching and learning and leads to power struggles over educational policy. Despite the potential for the phonics debate to polarize educational communities, most educators and parents try to avoid instructional pendulum swings that confuse rather than clarify issues. Rather, they choose to concentrate their efforts on providing effective literacy programs that are informed by the best research and practice available.

# CHAPTER 2

# How Readers and Writers Use Phonics

Long before they attempt to read and write, young children make use of *semantic cues* (meaning) and *syntactic cues* (grammar) to create meaning. If you said the following to a three-year-old: "I'm thinking of something I'd like for dinner and it's _____ ," the child might offer the following: *hot dogs, hamburgers, ice cream.* The word(s) the child gives undoubtedly would be something he or she had experienced or would like to experience for dinner and would fit syntactically, structurally, or grammatically in the slot provided. In other words, the child would respond to the meaning or semantic cues by only offering words that represent food. Similarly, a response such as *jumped* is highly unlikely. Even for a very young child, the sentence: "I'm thinking of something I'd like for dinner and it's *jumped*," would be unacceptable.  As speakers of English, children will offer words they think sound right in the open slot in the sentence. Thus, children offer grammatically appropriate nouns as they demonstrate sensitivity to the syntax of their language.

By the time children begin to read and write, they already have some knowledge of how oral language works. However, this does not alter their need for knowledge of sound-letter relationships; it simply means that they already have some important knowledge on which word identification strategies may be based.

# Common Word Identification Strategies for Reading

Reading is a highly complex process in which many sources of information are used to understand written texts, and young children bring a variety of information to the task of learning to read. By the time they enter first grade, most children have attained a high degree of control over their language. Even youngsters whose first language or dialect is not standard English have developed language systems that can be used as the basis for reading instruction. They not only have a high degree of control over the sounds of their language, they also possess large vocabularies, including words that name the content of their world and represent complex sets of meanings, and they have strategies for constructing a variety of simple and complex sentences. Their knowledge of oral language may be the most important thing that children bring to the task of learning to read. It serves as a foundation for learning the many conventions and features of printed language, such as directionality, spacing, and punctuation that are strange and new to beginning readers.

To identify words and comprehend written messages, readers use their knowledge of language and their personal experience as well as the print and pictures on the page. They employ strategies that make use of various code *cues* or prompts, which signal a particular tactic or combination of tactics for use in *decoding* (reading) or *encoding* (writing) messages in text. Decoding refers to the entire set of strategies readers use to "unlock the code," as shown in Figure 3. To most teachers and parents, however, the term decoding simply refers to the use of phonics to determine the pronunciation of words.

Some word identification strategies develop long before children are given formal instruction in reading. Emergent readers and writers use *environmental cues* from their everyday surroundings to signal what a word or group of words

| Figure 3 Strategies for Word Identification: Decoding | | |
|---|---|---|
| **Early strategies** | | **Ongoing strategies** |
| Make use of... | >>> | Make use of... |
| Environmental cues | give | Graphophonic (phonics) cues |
| Picture cues | way | Semantic (meaning) cues |
| Configuration (word form) cues | to | Syntactic (grammar/ sentence structure) cues |
| | >>> | Structural analysis (root words; word parts) |
| | | Background knowledge |

might be. Logos for fast–food restaurants are recognized by children as young as 2 years old. Many young children learn to read the word *STOP* on the traffic sign and, if they live in a high–rise apartment, they are likely to learn the words *up* and *down* from using the elevator. Whether children respond to the entire logo or to graphic cues on a particular word or letter, they often look quite phenomenal as they identify breakfast cereal brands and fast–food restaurants.

*Picture cues* offer another aid to word identification during children's very early years. Illustrations on a book or household product signal the written message to the reader. Later, when children begin formal instruction, they may be instructed to use illustrations only in conjunction with more relevant word identification strategies to decode an unknown word. Obviously, as children are confronted with an increasing amount of text and fewer illustrations, reliance on illustrations as a sole strategy for word identification loses its value.

*Configuration cues* also may be helpful to emerging readers and writers. Unusual visual patterns or unique letter forms, such as double letters in *little* or the letter *y* at the end of *baby*, may be sufficiently striking to cause young readers to remember them although their reading vocabularies still are very limited. However, like picture cues, configuration cues have short–term use.

As children move beyond the emergent stages of literacy and begin to approach reading and writing in a more formal way, knowledge of *graphophonic cues* (letters, letter clusters, and corresponding sounds) becomes essential. Thus, the use of phonics along with the use of context or semantic cues, syntactic cues, and broader textual meanings, become important interrelated strategies for word identification. Because of their interrelated nature, graphophonics, semantics, and syntax are commonly referred to as the *three cueing systems* of reading.

A reader's *background knowledge* plays a major role in the use of context clues. Even the very best decoder may miss the message if the content is outside his or her experience. For example, a child who gets stuck on the word *davenport* in the sentence, *Mary sat down to rest on the davenport*, may have no difficulty pronouncing all the words, but may remain unaware that Mary was resting on a couch.

Finally, *structural analysis cues* involve the use of structural elements in words to identify them. As mentioned earlier, this includes inflectional endings (–s, –ed, –ing), prefixes and suffixes (pre–, un–, –tion,), root words (*play*ful, *play*mate), and compound words (*raincoat, airplane*). Regardless of the word recognition strategies used, readers must verify their identification of an unfamiliar word by *cross checking* to determine whether or not it fits the context. If the word does not make sense, the reader must try another strategy. For example, in the sentence, *Without his gloves, John's hands were cold*, a young reader might use semantic cues for cross checking purposes in order to identify the word *gloves*, which does not fit the vowel generalization rule for words of this type. One consequence of cross checking is metacognitive, or conscious, awareness of the success of word identification (Fox, 1996).

The use of *word families, phonograms*, or *spelling patterns* (for example, *at* in b*at*, f*at*, c*at*) has been validated in several research efforts as an important strategy for identifying words (Goswami & Bryant, 1990; Moustafa, 1995; Treiman, 1985). Both children and adults find it more effective to divide syllables into their *onsets* (all letters before the vowel) and *rimes* (the vowel and what follows) than into any other units. Thus, the word *bat* is more easily divided into *b-at* than into *ba-t* or *b-a-t*. This research has led some to suggest that young children are likely to rely on their knowledge of onsets and rimes rather than rely on their knowledge of individual letters and related sounds to pronounce unfamiliar words. According to Moustafa (1997), children move from whole to parts: (1) They learn whole print words in which they remember the letters and the pronunciation together; (2) as they learn to recognize more and more print words, they encounter some with like letters or letter strings representing like onsets or rimes (for example, *smiles* and *small*); (3) they begin to learn the pronunciation of the parts of those words (for example, *sm* is pronounced /sm/, *iles* is pronounced /ilz/, and *all* is pronounced /al/) and begin to figure out the parts of the words; and (4) finally, as they encounter unfamiliar print words (such as *smart* and *tiles*), they make analogies at the onset–rime level. Children's use of onset–rime analogy provides new understandings about how young children learn to read the English language, which is both an onset–rime and alphabetic system. Emphasis on this strategy has shown particular promise for students who have failed in their initial attempts to learn to read (Gaskins, Ehri, Cress, O'Hara, & Donnelly, 1996–1997).

> **I**n addition to providing a window on the growth of children's phonetic knowledge, invented spelling during writing is increasingly seen as possessing reading instructional value as well.
> (Cunningham & Cunningham, 1992, p. 107)

## Phonics and Spelling

Writers use phonics to aid them in spelling the words they use to communicate ideas. Although most experienced writers spell with ease and accuracy, young writers find correct spelling to be one of the most challenging aspects of writing. Young writers have been known to change their text in order to accommodate their spelling needs. A teacher shared a story about a child who asked for help in spelling the word *piano*. He was writing the sentence, *My mother loves to play piano*. The teacher encouraged him to try spelling it on his own, only to discover later that he had revised the sentence to read, *My mother loves to play ball*. Effective teachers are aware of the need to provide an environment in which students feel comfortable enough to take risks in applying what they know. Children are fortunate when they have frequent opportunities for self-expression through writing such as the example shown in Figure 4 on page 20. These are students who grow in their awareness of phonics rules and gain greater control over them.

For many years, it was thought that learning to read was a prerequisite to learning to write and spell. In fact, attention to young children's writing is relatively recent. However, observations of preschool children in settings where they are encouraged to write independently reveal that many begin to develop strategies for spelling based on their knowledge of the phonological system and their knowledge of letter names (Read, 1971, 1975). Figure 4 shows how a kindergarten child makes use of his knowledge of letters and sounds to label his picture. As spellers become more experienced with written language, they learn to combine their knowledge of sound–letter relationships, their visual memories of how words look, and their morphemic knowledge (that is, their knowledge of words and word parts) to spell the words they need. A *morpheme* is the smallest unit of meaning in written language. Children build their knowledge of morphemes through abundant exposure to print and through direct instruction. For example, the *ed* in *wanted* and *ma* in *grandma* both are morphemic units. The chart shown in Figure 5 on page 21 helps to explain how even very young writers use these spelling strategies.

**Figure 4  Picture and Example of Invented Spelling of a Kindergarten Child**

SMP

Child: I am swimming in the pool.

Kindergarten (May)

Children's early independent spelling is sometimes referred to as *invented spelling, temporary spelling, constructive spelling, developmental spelling,* or *phonics-based spelling.* At first, these early spellings are the result of a child's natural encounters with print. Later, spellings become more and more conventional as children are increasingly exposed to written language and as they apply what they learn through

> ### Figure 5  Common Spelling Strategies Used by Beginning Writers
>
> **Sound-letter knowledge**: *I think I know which letters go with the sounds I hear.*
> Examples: (1) I think *ball* starts like /b/ in Billy's name. The last part rhymes with *call.*
>
> (2) From the way *crash* sounds, I think it begins with *cr.*
> I hear /a/ in the middle, so there must be an *a*, and it sounds like it ends with *sh.*
>
> **Visual memory**: *I remember how that word looks.*
> Examples: (1) I remember the word *puppy* has two *p*'s in the middle of the word, not just one.
>
> (2) The word *friend* does not fit the rules, but I remember how it looks in the middle.
>
> **Knowledge of words and word parts**: *I can use something I know about other words or parts of words to help me spell this one.*
> Examples: (1) *Rice* is almost like *mice*. I simply need to change the beginning.
>
> (2) I can change the end of *looks* to spell *looking.*

both informal and formal instruction. There appears to be no rigid sequence of development that all children follow as they learn to spell. In Figure 6 on pages 22–24, Powell and Hornsby (1993) describe three categories of development that show what might be expected when children apply what they know about written language and phonics as they spell. Obviously the writing of any individual child may include a variety of spelling behaviors across the three categories.

# Making the Best Use of Phonics

Good readers automatically recognize words that they encounter regularly. They do this by using their knowledge of letters and sounds, as well as by selecting and combining a variety of other strategies for word identification. Good writers use phonics in much the same way. Because

## Figure 6  Three Categories of Development

### EMERGENT SPELLERS

*Emergent spellers* understand the function of print. They begin to use print to communicate meaning, but they don't have sufficient graphophonic knowledge to communicate a message through writing alone because they use predominantly temporary spellings.

**Observations:**

- uses letter—like symbols
- no indication that child has:
1. letter knowledge
2. letter/sound correspondences
3. sense of wordness
- has idea that print carries message

Three Billy Goats Gruff, but there are six.

**Observations:**

- uses both initial and final sounds of words
- several conventional spellings
- capitalized *I* in second use
- uses dash to indicate letters missing
- uses some vowels
- word segmentation not evident

I was at the school today and I went to the gym today.

*(continued)*

**Figure 6  Three Categories of Development (continued)**

## NOVICE SPELLERS

*Novice spellers* have enough graphophonic knowledge to communicate meaning to others, but they use temporary spelling when writing unknown words and sometimes even when writing words they have frequently written before. They predominantly use phonic strategies for spelling.

**Observations:**

- word segmentation
- may need assistance with placement on page
- uses vowels consistently
- uncertainty of some spelling patterns (such as *sh*)
- uses primarily uppercase letters

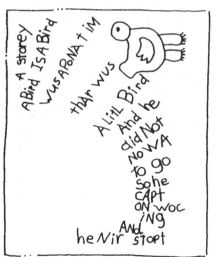

RYAN

A GOST is A
BAD SPERIT
YOU CAN FiD
HEM iN A
H+EDHAOZ SO
YOU HOD NOt
GO iN +o it

**Observations:**

- most sounds represented with reasonable letter/sounds
- many conventionally spelled words
- word segmentation used
- spacing on page may need attention
- mixes lowercase and uppercase
- vowels used consistently in each syllable

A storey
A Bird ISA Bird
wus A RONA+ iM
thar wus
A Litl Bird
And he
did Not
No WA
to go
So he
CApt
oN woc
iNG
And
he Nir stopt

  *(continued)*

**Figure 6  Three Categories of Development (continued)**

## INDEPENDENT SPELLERS

*Independent spellers* use conventional spelling for most words frequently written, and they have developed efficient strategies for spelling unknown words. They have also developed proofreading strategies.

**Observations:**

- mostly correct spelling
- knows hyphenated vowels and contractions
- mixes lower- and uppercase letters
- uses letter format
- needs attention on punctuation and capitals

> Dear Scott
>
> I hope you get to Be A Teacher THiS is my First Time To Be A pen-Pal And iS FUn Being youer peh-Pal. if you Are My Teacher Then you'll Be As good As Any Other Teacher. I hAve to puppies do you have Any PeTs
>
> from you'er pen-PAl
>
> DAVid

**Observations:**

- mostly correct spelling
- knows hyphenated words, compound words
- spells plural forms
- proofreading skills not apparent

> Dress-Up
>
> I like to dress up with Jennifer. We put on fancy dresses and gloves and very pretty Purses. We put on high hill shoes. And We put on Make up And we like to play house with the dresses. Some day I with that I can wear every thing in Public, but I dought it.
>
> The End

## Figure 7  Suggested Guidelines for Learning and Teaching Phonics

- Teaching phonics is *not* synonymous with teaching reading.
- Reading and spelling require much more than phonics.
- Phonics is a means to an end, not the end itself.
- Phonics is one of several enablers or cueing systems that help us read.
- Phonics is one of several strategies for spelling.
- Memorizing phonics rules does not ensure application of those rules.
- Learners need to see the relevance of phonics for themselves in their own reading and writing.
- Teaching students to use phonics is different from teaching them *about* phonics.
- The best context for learning and applying phonics is actual reading and writing.

our writing system is alphabetic, the use of sound–letter knowledge is a logical strategy for gaining independence as a reader and writer. It always must be kept in mind, however, that phonics does not stand alone. It is used during reading and spelling and its use is informed by reading and spelling. In other words, readers use what they learn about phonics during writing, and writers are helped to spell by what they have learned about phonics through reading. Phonics is influenced greatly by the language context in which it is applied. It is reasonable to assume that young readers and writers who have a range of word identification strategies will make the best use of phonics. Figure 7 offers some guidelines, based on research and experience, for use in helping children learn phonics.

Phonics and its role in learning to read is a topic that is highly controversial and often is misunderstood. It is frequently used as a catch–all term to stand for a return to the "basics." This is particularly true when students' achievement in reading does not meet expectations. Many educators, whether they are new or experienced, are attempting to become better informed about phonics and its role in providing a balanced and effective reading program.

# CHAPTER 3

# How Have Changes in Literacy Instruction Influenced the Teaching of Phonics?

New insights into learning and teaching have produced numerous changes in the ways reading and writing are taught. Among the most noticeable changes are (1) greater emphasis on writing and its relation to reading; (2) greater use of trade books and library books; (3) increased attention to the integration of the language arts; and (4) greater reliance on informal classroom assessment. Following is a brief description of each change and how it affects literacy instruction in general and phonics in particular.

## Greater Emphasis on Writing and Its Relation to Reading

Until the 1980s, very little attention was given to writing instruction during the elementary years (Graves, 1983). Handwriting always has been stressed in elementary classrooms, but attention to the composition of stories and expository texts was quite limited. Things have changed. Even the youngest students now are given opportunities to communicate through written language on a daily basis. Teachers emphasize the processes involved, including selecting and framing a topic, creating and revising drafts, and editing, so that what is written may be shared with others. Teachers of young children are aware that children's attempts to write encourage their interest in and need for the alphabetic code. Thus, much of today's phonics instruction takes place during writing. Phonics is linked to reading as a tool for word identification and to writing as a tool for spelling.

## Teachers No Longer Treat Copying as Writing

Until the 1980s, much of what a child wrote in first grade consisted of copying from a chalkboard. The material may have been composed by the class, but more often it was composed by the teacher and then read in unison by the class before it was copied. Teachers emphasized handwriting and neatness (see Figure 8 on page 28). It was generally assumed that children needed a fairly substantial spelling vocabulary and some word recognition skills before they could be expected to compose their own material. Even then, a heavy emphasis was placed on mechanical correctness of written language, and little attention was given to the content or the act of composing. Because children's writing tended to be restricted only to what they could write without errors, it consisted primarily of short, highly prosaic sentences much like those they normally copied from the board.

What does the child whose work is in Figure 8 know about written language? Josh knows how to copy successfully from the board and forms letters correctly and neatly. He may have an understanding of the concept of space between words in written language. It cannot be assumed that Josh is able to read back what he copied.

Today is Friday.
It is raining.
Monday is the birthday of
Martin Luther King.
                Josh
                Grade 1

## Teachers Now Encourage Beginning Readers and Writers to Make Personal Attempts at Writing

From the earliest grades, today's students are encouraged to communicate through writing (see Figure 9). Because they may have had the benefit of only a minimum amount of instruction in reading and writing, they can be expected to make mistakes. The mistakes they make usually are quite inventive and informing because children use their knowledge about written language to give as close an approximation to conventional spelling as they can. Keep in mind that *these attempts do not replace deliberate instruction in phonics*. However, opportunities to write are an important part of this instruction. Through a series of mutually supportive opportunities for both direct and indirect instruction, children use phonics to develop skill in spelling and competence in their ability to communicate effectively through writing.

What does the child whose work is in Figure 9 know about written language? First and most important, this child knows how to express her personal ideas through her own independent writing. Tiesha knows that in written language there are spaces between words. She is beginning to understand the use of capital letters at the beginning of a sentence and a period at the end. She has command of the sound–letter relationship of *p* in both the initial and medial position of the word *people*. Other consonant sound–letter relationships she uses correctly are represented by *b* in *because*; *th* in *they're*; *s* in *same*; *d, f,* and *t* in *different*; and *c* in *color*. She has correctly spelled the word *wood*, but needs help with the homophone (*wood/would*). She correctly uses the in-

---

### Figure 9  Example of a First-Grade Student Communicating Through Writing

Responding to literature about Martin Luther King, Jr., which was read aloud by her teacher and discussed by her first-grade class, Tiesha wrote:

I HAVE A DREAM THAT SOMEDAY . . .

Piepl wood stop fteing
(People would stop fighting)

becoa's ther the sam
(because they're the same)

ther jaut's derfit colers.
(they're just different colors.)

Tiesha M.
Grade 1

flectional ending *ing*. (The lack of an *e* at the end of the word *same* indicates that Tiesha may be ready for attention to the vowel generalization regarding the *e* marker at the end of short words of this type (first vowel is long; *e* is silent). She uses conventional spellings for the words *stop* and *the*. It is likely that Tiesha can read what she wrote.

## Greater Use of Trade Books and Library Books

Concern over the use of bland, unmotivating texts for reading instruction, coupled with the availability of more high-quality children's books, led to the introduction of trade books in beginning reading instruction. Although the use of such materials does not preclude a strong phonics emphasis, teachers using trade books as core materials are more likely to capitalize on the opportunities for phonics instruction presented in the literature rather than rely on a rigidly applied hierarchy of skills. Many teachers attempt to blend both approaches by selecting literature that contains the elements they want to teach and then teach them in a *planful* manner. In either case, emphasis is placed on learning phonics in combination with other word identification skills in a context that stimulates children's desire to read. In order to understand the changes that have occurred in the kinds of materials used to teach phonics, it is helpful to have some further background on phonics and instructional materials.

### Phonics and Instructional Materials

Basal readers produced during the latter part of the 20th century include organized phonics programs. However, because many of these programs made use of a small foundational vocabulary taught as sight words, their approach is termed by some as the *sight-word* or *whole-word method*. According to Heilman (1989) these terms are misnomers, because no current method or philosophy of reading instruction advocates a total sight- or whole-word approach. Although traditional basal readers included phonics instruction, they differed as to the point at which phonics was first introduced, the degree of emphasis on phonics, and the type of phonics used. Differences of this type remain true of today's literature-based, core reading, and language arts programs as well.

Although there are many ways to approach phonics, two different approaches tended to dominate materials and practice in the past. *Synthetic phonics* refers to an approach in which the sounds identified with letters are learned in isolation and blended together. Children are taught to segment a single syllable word such as *cat* into three parts /c/a/t/ and to blend the parts together to form a word. A multisyllable word might be segmented as follows: al/pha/bet. *Analytic phonics* refers to an approach in which the sounds associated with letters are not pronounced in isolation. Children identify the phonic element from a set of words in which each word contains the particular element under study. For example, teacher and students discuss how the following words are alike: *pat, park, push,* and *pen.* Analytic phonics is used in the example given earlier in which a typical basal phonics lesson is described.

> **The child with limited reading skills and low general ability will build vocabulary and cognitive structures through immersion in literacy actuates just as his or her high-achieving counterpart does. (Stanovich, 1994, p. 282)**

Much of the controversy surrounding traditional basal reading programs and phonics centers on disagreements about which of the two approaches, synthetic or analytic, is better. Those who favor instruction with a heavy emphasis on phonics lean toward an explicit or synthetic approach. Many school districts select core reading and language arts programs based on the amount and type of phonics instruction included. The controversy has expanded beyond the type of phonics taught to include issues related to the intensity of instructional delivery and sequence of instruction.

Many teachers purchase supplementary phonics programs to accompany their core literacy programs. Ironically, some teachers may unwittingly contribute to the word recognition problems of marginal students by, for example, pairing a core program using analytic phonics with a supplementary program that uses synthetic phonics. Teachers also may pair a program in which letter names are taught and linked to the sounds they represent with one in which the letters actually are identified by the sounds they represent. For example, teaching that the letter *b* represents the sound *buh* is quite different from actually calling that letter *buh* rather than its letter name. Thus, an instructional mismatch is created that may confuse the children for whom the heavy emphasis on phonics was intended to help.

Beyond the initial levels of reading, traditional basal programs introduced books in the elementary grades that contained stories in which the vocabulary was highly controlled and through which specific language elements were taught in a highly sequenced manner. Teachers often organized primary–grade reading instruction around three ability groups, which allowed students to proceed through the material at varying rates. Assessment consisted primarily of multiple–choice tests given at the completion of each book. Skills such as phonics generally were monitored through worksheet activities.

Following are descriptions that contrast the teaching of phonics as an isolated skill unlinked to meaningful text with the teaching of phonics as a tool grounded in familiar and meaningful text and as part of the entire reading process.

| Figure 10  Text From a Traditional First-Grade Basal Reader |
| --- |
| See Jack go. <br> Go, go Jack. <br> Jack can go fast. |

## Teachers Are Moving Away From Total Reliance on Tightly Controlled, Highly Contrived Texts to Teach Reading

Many adults in the United States learned to read from text such as that shown in Figure 10. Traditional basal readers contained highly controlled vocabulary in stories written for a particular reading series. Books at the beginning levels, preprimers and primers, were designed to introduce children to a limited number of words, which were repeated in several stories. Although the early basals of the 1940s and 1950s included little or no phonics, basals since that time have made use of *sight words* (words taught as wholes for instant recognition) as the basis for the introduction of phonics. After children had mastered a limited sight vocabulary, sight words and phonics continued to be taught side-by-side. Most basal phonics programs began by teaching a few consonants in the initial position. Because consonants are much more consistent in their relations to sounds than are vowels, those that represent only one sound (such as *m, n, p, b, h,* and *w*) usually were taught early in a sequence of instruction. Having introduced a few such consonants, instruction also would include final consonants, vowels, and structural elements. Although there was a conscious effort to link the phonics lessons to the reading material, these lessons often were taught in a manner that was isolated from real reading. Following are some key elements of a typical phonics lesson that might have occurred within the more eclectic basal readers of the 1970s, 1980s, or 1990s, or in a program used in conjunction with such readers.

**Visual discrimination and letter recognition.** The teacher displays the upper- and lower-case forms of the letter under consideration. For example, a key letter card with the letters *Ww* is displayed. Children are told that this is the letter *w* and they are asked to repeat the name of the letter. In some cases, they also may be asked to use paper and pencil to form or trace the letter.

**Auditory discrimination.** The children are shown a key picture card with the picture of something that begins with the /w/ sound. For example, a picture of a wagon might be used. With heavy stress on the initial sound /w/ in *wagon*, the children are told that the word *wagon* begins with the letter *w*. They are asked to repeat the word in unison and to notice how their lips form at the beginning of the word. Words from their basal vocabulary list such as *we* and *was* also are recalled and compared. A variety of auditory discrimination games might follow. For example, the teacher might say a list of words and ask whether they begin like *wagon*, *was*, and *we*. In most cases, the teacher would not attempt to isolate the sound of the letter *w*, because it cannot be isolated without distortion. The teacher places emphasis on helping children hear and see the similarity in a given set of words or pictures that stand for words. The goal is for students to become familiar with a specific sound-letter relationship and generalize this knowledge for new situations.

**Application.** A worksheet with pictures of various objects is distributed to the children. Students are asked to mark all the items that begin with the same sound as the word *wagon*.

**Extension.** Additional activities might include cutting and pasting pictures of items that begin with the /w/ sound-letter relationship. In addition, a review of all the phonics elements taught would take place over time, both through oral activities and through an abundance of paper and pencil practice tasks.

**Assessment.**  Paper and pencil tasks of the type described earlier are used for both instruction and ongoing assessment.

## Today's Teachers of Beginning Reading Are Moving Toward the Use of Patterned Texts Containing Humor and Lively Illustrations

A good example of a book for use with beginning readers is *I Went Walking* by Sue Williams, a picture book containing repetitive vocabulary and language patterns (see Figure 11 on page 36). It is beautifully illustrated, simple, and humorous. On the following page are key points in a series of lessons that might be used with materials of this type.

*Students working with a beginning consonants game.*

Figure 11 Text That Can Be Used With Beginning Readers

I went walking.
What did you see?
I saw a black cat looking at me.

I went walking.
What did you see?
I saw a brown horse looking at me.
(from the book *I Went Walking* by Sue Williams)

**Modeling.** Through numerous shared readings of the book, children are invited to participate as the teacher reads aloud to them. They join in on repeated words and sentences. Children notice how the teacher turns the pages and how his or her hand occasionally sweeps from left to right or top to bottom, indicating where the written message is located and the direction in which his or her eyes are moving.

**Repeated readings and response.** Children respond to repeated readings of the text in a variety of ways, such as discussion, drama, and drawing and writing.

**Identifying textual features.** After several readings, children are guided to look more closely at the textual features. They may match sentences in the book with sentences the teacher has written on a strip of oak tag. They may reconstruct sentences that have been cut into individual words.

**Phonics.** As children become more familiar with the text, they are guided to notice the words beginning with the letter *w* that are repeated throughout the book in the sentences *I went walking. What did you see?* They match the words visually, read them in unison, and discuss the sound–letter relationship.

**Using the language of literacy.** Throughout these activities, both teacher and children use the language of literacy. Vocabulary such as letter, word, sentence, period, author, and illustrator are used in context, so that students attain the vocabulary needed to learn and talk about what they read and write.

**Application.** Whole-group activities using the Big Book version of texts such as *I Went Walking* are accompanied by opportunities for independent reading of the smaller version of the Big Book at school and at home. Children also are engaged in many traditional phonics activities with the letter *w* such as creating a chart of pictures of things that begin with the letter *w*. Through daily independent writing opportunities, such as journal writing or written responses to literature, children are encouraged to apply all the sound–letter relationships that have been taught.

**Assessment.** Assessment is highly integrated with instruction. Ongoing informal classroom assessment of children's participation in whole-group activities and their independent reading and writing helps determine the children who need additional help. Children are held accountable for skills and strategies that have been addressed through direct and indirect instruction. Teachers also look for evidence of students' risk taking as they attempt to apply what they have learned to sound–letter relationships that have not been addressed specifically. Teachers are less concerned with teaching each specific letter in a particular sequence than in helping children develop an awareness of the alphabetic principle and an understanding of how this knowledge can help them read and write. Emphasis is placed on guiding children to make their own personal discoveries of how their language system works so that they can use this knowledge to generalize to new situations. That is, the ultimate goal is to teach so that students can use what they have learned in similar but new contexts.

The key differences between this lesson and the one described earlier in the chapter is that this lesson grounds instruction in authentic literature and requires students to use the phonics element being studied in a meaningful and strategic manner. This lesson also could be described as a blend of implicit (or embedded) instruction with explicit instruction. Making use of a whole–to–part–to–whole framework, described in Figure 12 on page 43, the teacher begins by immersing children in examples of the pattern underlying the skill or strategy they are studying (the letter *w* sound–symbol relationship) in the hope that they will begin to discover it on their own. However, whether or not they discover the pattern themselves, students are guided to look closely at how it exists in whole text. Once the pattern is discussed, it is removed from the context and is given more intense and explicit scrutiny. Finally, students are given opportunities to use what they know about the pattern in their reading and spelling and they are held accountable for it. The teacher is given an opportunity to discover whether children have truly learned what has been taught and to tailor future lessons accordingly.

> **All children use phonics to read. The truth is that some attention to the relationships between spelling patterns and their pronunciations is characteristic of all types of reading programs, including whole language. (Stahl, 1992, p. 618).**

Many teachers now are creating their own programs of instruction, selecting the literature themselves, and offering phonics instruction much like the series of lessons described in this chapter. This trend also is reflected in some commercially prepared materials for beginning reading. However, in an attempt to please a wide variety of consumers, publishers of literature–based programs are likely to include options that reflect more than one approach to teaching phonics. They may differ, however, in the amount of phonics offered prior to actual book–reading experiences. Programs that espouse a "phonics first" approach will expose children to heavy doses of intensive phonics before much instruction is offered with books and stories. This is in contrast to programs in which phonics is more closely linked to the literature selections that children read from the beginning. For the most part, however, commercially prepared materials are less likely to reflect one strong philosophical base, because their goal is to provide something for everyone. Whether teacher prepared or commercially published, there is one thing of which you can be assured: Today's reading programs will include phonics.

## Increased Attention to the Integration of the Language Arts

Research into the nature of language learning has caused many to change their view of language as a complex system in which the parts are both integrated and interdependent. When an individual component is isolated from the written language system, it no longer functions as it does within real reading and writing. The interdependent nature of the elements of language becomes highly evident when phonics rules are applied too rigidly. For example, the letter string *r-e-a-d* is pronounced very differently depending on the context in which it is presented: "Yesterday, I *read* the entire sports page; I hope I'll have time to *read* today's as well." The rule that applies here states that when two vowels are side by side, the long sound of the first one is heard and the second usually is silent. Clymer (1963/1996) reported on the utility of 45 phonic generalizations. Many elementary teachers were shocked to learn that this widely taught generalization about two vowels side by side was listed as having 309 conforming words (such as *bead*) and 377 exceptions (such as *chief*), so it was useful less than 50% of the time. As one teacher put it, "Mr. Clymer, for years I've been teaching 'When two vowels go walking, the first one does the talking.' You're ruining the romance in the teaching of reading!" (p. 187).

The fact that most of the phonic generalizations taught in elementary school are not valid much of the time does not suggest that they should never be taught. In addition to the rule cited earlier, the following vowel generalizations generally are considered useful for primary–grade students: (1) When there are two vowels in a word, one of which is final *e*, the first vowel is long and the final *e* is silent (63%); and (2) When a vowel is in the middle of a one–syllable word, the vowel usually is short (62%). Teachers should avoid teaching these generalizations as rules to be memorized; rather, they should be taught as examples of language patterns that may be put to strategic use for reading and spelling. Most important, teachers should be aware of studies such as Clymer's in order to make instructional decisions based on what will be most useful to students and to anticipate potential confusion and difficulty. This research speaks to the need to provide students with multiple word recognition strategies. Overreliance on any one strategy, including phonics, actually may hinder young readers and writers. They need to learn early that the pronunciation and meaning of words are influenced not only by the way they look, but by the language context in which they are found.

## Teachers Are Moving Away From Teaching the Language Arts—Listening, Speaking, Reading, and Writing—as Discrete Entities

During the 1930s, the organizational pattern in which children were placed in long–term groups according to ability emerged as the preferred approach to addressing individual differences in reading ability. Listening, speaking, and writing were addressed separately and were given less instructional emphasis than reading. Spelling was taught as a discrete subject totally unrelated to writing. When spelling was considered within the context of writing, it was largely to note errors. Little was done to help students self–edit for spelling or make note of the kinds of spelling errors made during writing. Even phonics can be taught as a distinct activity separate from the time spent reading books in small groups. Rather than be introduced to sound–letter relationships as textual patterns found in familiar literature, most teachers taught these relations in a particular sequence and in isolation from real text. For this type of instruction, teachers made use of phonics kits or workbook exercises and employed a whole–group instructional format. Although many children successfully applied what was learned, many others failed to make the connection between phonics and its application to reading or spelling.

With so much emphasis given to phonics as an isolated subject, some students tended to rely almost exclusively on phonics, making little use of other word recognition strategies that might, if used in combination with phonics, help them to make better use of what they knew about sound–letter relationships. Students were subjected to large amounts of phonics whether they needed it or did not. Children who already were reading were likely to get the same amount of phonics instruction as those who arrived at school with relatively few prior experiences at home with books and print. Children with limited exposure to print might receive heavy phonics instruction before they had sufficient understandings about print to facilitate its application.

> Only when we can comprehend the whole are we fully able to see how the parts relate to it. Kids who can read are usually good at learning phonics, because they can put phonic relationships into the context of making sense of print. (Goodman, 1993, p. 85)

## Teachers Are Moving Toward Organizing Language Arts Instruction Around Large Blocks of Time in Which Oral Language and Written Language Are Taught in an Integrated Way

A growing number of teachers have devoted a specific block of their teaching day to emphasize language arts. In the primary grades, this might be as much as 90 minutes or more. A large part of this time is devoted to reading instruction. However, strong connections are made with writing and oral language by using whole texts to identify specific aspects of language for in-depth study. Specific strategies addressed include those that make use of phonemic awareness, phonics, or structural analysis along with aspects of reading comprehension and the writing process. Phonics is linked to both reading and spelling. Its knowledge provides the basis of one of several word recognition strategies; for example, the use of semantics or meaning (Does that word make sense?) can confirm phonics when applied to an unknown word.

Children are encouraged to do a great deal of independent reading and writing in which they are urged to apply what they have learned. For example, the child described earlier who experienced the series of lessons with the letter *w* would be expected to begin the spelling of the word *water* even if he or she could not spell much of the rest of the word. Children are held accountable for what they are taught. They are encouraged to use prior knowledge to make attempts to figure out what they may not know. Gradually, as they gain experience and receive more instruction, their spelling becomes more conventional and their reading more fluent. Figure 12 depicts how a teacher might conceptualize a lesson or series of lessons that attempt to help students look at the parts of language in the context of the whole. Children are exposed to examples of the language element to be studied. The examples are embedded in whole text and then extracted for closely guided scrutiny. As students scrutinize the parts of language being studied, they are encouraged to form generalizations, find other examples, and discuss any "rules" that they can derive. This part of the lesson makes use of many traditional methods of teaching skills. Finally, students are asked to apply what they know using meaningful, whole texts. This may involve rereading familiar texts or creating new ones.

## Figure 12  Blending Skills With Meaning: A Whole-to-Part-to-Whole Conceptual Framework

WHOLE ————to————PART ————to———— WHOLE

| | | |
|---|---|---|
| Learning *with, through,* and *about* whole written texts.* | Learning *about* the parts of written language texts. | Applying what was learned *with, through,* and *about* whole written language texts. |

Examples of activities

| *whole* | *part* | *whole* |
|---|---|---|
| *Reading/writing aloud* Teacher models, students observe and respond. | *Direct instruction* focuses on selected elements from whole text. | *Rereading* Familiar texts |

*Includes*

| *Shared reading/writing* Teacher leads; students participate to the extent they can. | Phonemic Awareness Sound/letter patterns for onsets and rimes Phonics Structural Analysis *and* Other Word Recognition Strategies | *Writing* Creating alternative texts Response to reading |
|---|---|---|
| *Guided reading/writing* Teacher engages students in systematic manner with closely guided support. | (Focus on patterns in sentences, words, word parts, letters, and sounds.) | *Reading* Applies to new/similar texts (Help is given as needed. Application is monitored.) |

*Whole texts include predictable stories, dictated stories, content–area materials, letters, charts of songs, rhymes, messages, lists, and so on.

Adapted from Strickland, D.S. (1989). *Teaching skills in a literature-based classroom.* Workshop handout distributed at the 34th Annual Convention of the International Reading Association, New Orleans, LA.

# Greater Reliance on Informal Classroom Assessment

Although many still consider standardized tests the chief indicator of student achievement, classroom teachers are beginning to make greater use of informal assessment procedures to inform them about student progress. Teachers have come to realize that standardized tests tell them very little about a specific child's strengths and weaknesses. These tests usually are given at the end of the year, rendering the results useless for instructional purposes. Some teachers complain that standardized tests do not accurately reflect what they have emphasized instructionally. Still others observe that young children sometimes are overwhelmed by the format of these tests, which often is very different from the kinds of literacy materials they use on a daily basis. Teachers have gathered evidence from workbooks and worksheets, but this too is not always satisfactory, because some children can function well on these materials and still have difficulty applying skills. Still others can read with fluency and meaning, but have difficulty with worksheets (Yuill & Oakhill, 1991). Today's teachers seek to obtain information about how students use word identification tools, such as phonics, when they are involved in reading and writing for their own purposes. They are aware that the best test of knowledge is its application during use. Observing children's application of phonics is the best indicator of how well they have learned it.

## Teachers Are Moving Away From a Reliance on Standardized Tests and Other Commercially Prepared Assessment Tools

For many years, the primary way to evaluate how well students had learned phonics was through a demonstration of knowledge about sound–letter relationships. Most often this was done by observing performance during instructional activities and on worksheets like the one shown in Figure 13. To be sure, when a child circles the letter *d* under a picture of a dog to indicate the sound it represents at the beginning, we know that this child is making some very valuable connections. It tells us little, however, about the child's ability to use this information in the act of reading and writing. Teachers have observed that children's re-

## Figure 13  Sample Phonics Worksheet

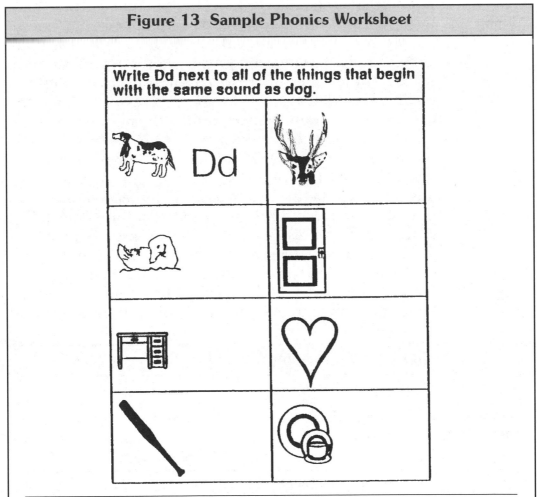

From *Language, Literacy and the Child*, Second Edition, by Lee Galda, Bernice E. Cullinan, and Dorothy S. Strickland, copyright ©1997, 1993 by Harcourt Brace and Company. Reprinted by permission of the publisher.

quirements on skills sheets can pose a very different challenge from the strategic use of phonics required when they actually read and write.

## Teachers Are Moving Toward the Use of Teacher-Prepared, Ongoing Assessment Strategies

Many school districts have reduced the number of norm–referenced tests given before third grade. These have been replaced by a variety of performance-based assessment procedures that are linked closely to the curriculum. For example, teachers may use some form of running record of the types of errors children make during oral reading (see Clay, 1989). This type of assessment helps the teacher go beyond merely recording the number of errors made to making note of the *type* of errors made. For example, when a child makes a reading error, it may be due to a lack of attention to one of several cues to word recognition. In Figure 14, the reader says *call* for *calm*, indicating a lack of attention to what makes sense in this context. Use of the word *came* also should signal a sense of discomfort in the reader; it neither makes sense nor is its use "the way we say it" (English sentence structure) in our language. *Clean* for *calm* indicates use of the visual elements in *calm* in an attempt to apply phonics. But, the learner must go beyond

| Figure 14  All Reading Errors Are Not Equal | | |
|---|---|---|

Example:
A picture of a mother bathing a child is accompanied by the following sentence:
*Mother tried to* calm *the crying baby.*

| Error | Possible prompt | Type of error |
|---|---|---|
| *call* for *calm* | semantic (meaning) | Does that make sense? |
| *came* for *calm* | syntax (sentence structure) | Does that sound right? |
| *clean* for *calm* | graphophonic (sound–letter) | It could be, but look again. |

the visual and think in terms of what makes sense and what sounds correct in our language. The type of errors readers make will suggest the type of prompts that should be offered and will determine the kind of follow-up instruction required.

Observing and monitoring children's attempts at spelling during writing is another invaluable window into their ability to use phonics. The analysis in Figure 9 on page 29 is an example of how a teacher might assess phonics within the instructional context. Teachers look for the application of skills already taught as well as attempts that go beyond the instruction already received. This helps to indicate what a child is ready for next. Work samples of this type also provide specific, concrete evidence for use during parent conferences. Today's teachers find it much more helpful to spend time with parents reviewing their child's work samples and records gleaned from checklists and observational notes than merely discussing standardized test results. Products and observations from instructional activities provide a vivid and accurate description of an individual's personal progress.

New insights into young children's literacy development have led to changes in beginning reading instruction. The insights not only stem from recent research, however, they also are grounded in research of the past that is now better understood and put to better use. For example, knowledge about the writing process and its relation to reading has led to new understandings about how young children's early writing can promote the development of phonics. It also reveals how children's attempts to spell can be used to monitor what they know about phonics as well as how they put this knowledge to use. Perhaps more than ever before, today's teachers are apt to blend phonics into an instructional framework that emphasizes the reader's construction of meaning with texts. In this way, students are encouraged to use phonics as a tool toward making sense of what they read rather than as an end in itself.

# CHAPTER 4

# Finding the Balance: Systematic, Intensive, Code-Driven Phonics Versus Holistic, Embedded, Meaning-Driven Approaches

The discussion of the controversies surrounding phonics is not complete without addressing the issues in their current and most extreme form—the debate surrounding systematic, intensive phonics versus holistically oriented approaches. This is the form in which the controversy most likely is to be cast to the general public. The distinction between these two approaches is most significant at the very earliest point of formal instruction in reading.

Stated briefly, educators who promote systematic, intensive phonics advocate an emphasis on phonics that is highly sequenced, skills or code–driven, and initiated early in the child's schooling. Children begin by learning about the parts of words and build toward whole words. Correct identification and automaticity of response is stressed. Much of the research cited to support this view is grounded in experimental studies in which children's demonstration of performance is based on the results of standardized tests (Adams, 1990; Chall, 1983).

Holistically oriented approaches include philosophies and practices frequently associated with terms such as whole language, integrated language arts, and literature-based curricula. In practice, these terms share certain characteristics; however, they are not synonymous. For example, the trends in literacy education outlined in Chapter 3: greater emphasis on writing and its relation to reading, greater use of trade books, increased attention to the integration of the language arts, and greater reliance on informal classroom assessment are visible in virtually all classrooms where a holistic orientation is espoused. However, implementation and adherence to various philosophies varies widely from teacher to teacher. To make matters more confusing, teachers who support intensive, systematic phonics often include some of the instructional elements considered to be holistic in nature.

In a discussion of phonics, the distinction between an explicit code or skills emphasis (systematic, intensive phon-

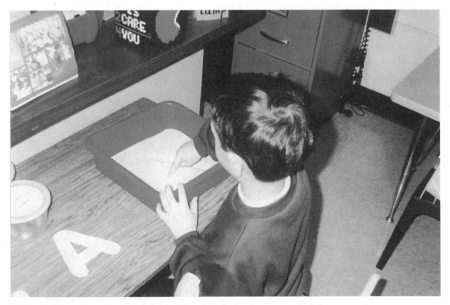

*A student tracing the letter A in the sand.*

ics) and an embedded code or meaning emphasis (read-ing- and writing-based phonics) rests in how reading is taught from the very beginning. Advocates of reading- and writing-based phonics focus on instruction that is embed-ded within the processes of learning to read and write and emphasize the child's ability to make meaning with text.

> **If the young reader is to work effectively on different kinds of texts he needs to have experience of texts of different types, for reading with understanding is more than reading words. (Clay, 1991, p. 291)**

Children begin with the use of whole texts involving shared literacy activities with an adult and move to the identification of phrases and words and the examination of word parts. Emphasis on meaning is main-tained even as children examine word parts, because the purpose is to help them see the patterns in the language so they can apply the knowledge to new situations. Those who endorse a meaning emphasis are likely to cite basic research on how children learn to read and write as well as classroom-based studies on long-term effects of reading- and writing-based phonics (Krashen, 1993; Weaver, 1994).

Recognizing that in most controversies there is something to be learned from both sides, this book has attempted to avoid extremes on the phonics debate. For example, educators on both sides of the debate agree that ultimately, reading and writing for meaning is paramount. Both sides are keenly aware of the importance of good lit-erature in the lives of children and the need for responsive adults who support children's natural inclinations toward making sense of print.

Both sides of the phonics debate could learn from ed-ucators in Finland. Because the Finnish language is said to be the most regular alphabetic writing system in use today (Venezky, 1973), it is not surprising that educators there turned to synthetic phonics as the major instructional ap-proach to beginning reading. It also is not surprising that Finnish researchers report that phonics instruction decreased poor readers' decoding problems in the first grade. "Even the students with low IQs can learn fluent mechanical reading skills" (Korkeamaki & Dreher, 1993, p. 478). However, the jump start in phonics given to Finnish children has not created a country free of reading problems. Studies suggest that a large proportion of Finnish children have serious problems with reading comprehension: 20% in Grade 3 (Vahapassi, 1977a); 50% in Grade 6 (Vahapassi, 1977b), and 30% in Grade 9 (Vahapassi, 1987). These findings parallel Venezky's (1973) finding that although Finnish students achieve a surprisingly high level of sound–letter mastery by the end of Grade 1, only 25% of the variation in the students' reading ability in the second and third grade could be attributed to the mastery of sound–letter correspondence. It could be that for many learners, an instructional program (in any discipline) that is devoid of meaning and purpose produces mindless, quick results at the expense of long-term strategies for independence and self-improvement. This should not be viewed as an indictment of phonics; rather, it is an indictment of how phonics was taught in this situation. The questions educators and parents face regarding phonics never has been about whether or not to teach it, but about how much phonics to teach, to whom, and at what time.

Educators who seek to provide a comprehensive and balanced instructional program would do well to consider the following:

- Instruction is systematic when it is planned, deliberate in application, and proceeds in an orderly manner. This does not mean a rigid progression of "one-size-fits-all" instruction. Rather, it means a thoughtfully planned program that takes into account learner variability.

- The intensity of instruction on any particular skill or strategy should be based on need. Thus, intensity will vary both with individuals and groups. There is no substitute for ongoing documentation and monitoring of learning in order to determine the level of intensity needed to help a child or group of children succeed in a particular area.

• The use of techniques to track specific goals and objectives within an integrated language arts framework is essential. Alignment of curricular goals with instructional planning and assessment helps provide everyone involved with a clear sense of direction. Instruction should be engaging and rich with meaning, yet grounded in curricular expectations that are visible to teachers, parents, students, and concerned others.

• Instructional techniques that help children understand and make use of the alphabetic code should be applied with those that guide students in reading comprehension, thoughtful response to literature, and the effective use of the writing process.

Avoiding instructional extremes is at the heart of providing a balanced program of reading instruction. However, finding the balance should not imply that there is a specific balanced approach. Nor should it suggest a sampling method in which "a little of this and a little of that" are mixed together to form a disparate grouping of approaches euphemistically termed "eclectic." Ultimately, instruction must be informed by how children learn and how they can best be taught. Achieving informed balance is an ongoing endeavor that requires knowledge, time, and thoughtfulness.

# CHAPTER 5

# Learning Phonics: Strategies That Support Beginning Readers and Writers

Learning phonics is not something children do in a vacuum. It occurs within the context of family and school environments that influence whether or not children are successful. Virtually all children come to school having had some exposure to print during their daily lives; however, the nature and extent of this exposure varies widely. It is no surprise that children's ability to learn phonics is related to the frequency and quality of their informal experiences with written and oral language. The concepts presented in this chapter provide a foundation for phonics and continue to develop along with phonics. Children begin to develop these concepts at home and in school settings with early-childhood caregivers and teachers. They learn best when the adults who care for them *plan* for the activities and experiences to happen in relatively informal and enjoyable ways rather than as a set of rigidly prescribed, formal lessons.

## Strategies for Developing the Foundations of Reading and Writing

*Print awareness* involves an understanding that reading and writing represent ideas, knowledge, and thoughts. Attention to print is an important first step toward developing an understanding of what it means to be a reader and writer, even though it may or may not predict an ease of understanding the relations between the sounds and symbols of written language. Adults promote children's print awareness by providing print rich environments and by being responsive to young children's questions and comments about print.

*Print concepts* are the arbitrary conventions that govern written language, such as spaces between words, directionality, and punctuation. Developing an understanding of how print works is essential to make sense of written language. Adults promote an understanding of print concepts when they move their hand from left to right while reading a familiar phrase or sentence, point to individual words to help children associate the spoken and written forms, call attention to the need to put spaces between words while

*A student creates a story at a literacy center.*

writing a note or list dictated by a child, and respond to children's questions about periods or question marks they have noticed during reading or writing.

*Functions of print* involves knowledge of how print is used for everyday purposes, such as writing notes and letters, reading newspapers and magazines, making and using lists, and using a television guide. Children who realize the functional relevance of written language are more likely to be motivated to explore its use for their own purposes. Adults include children in functional activities involving print, such as clipping coupons from a supermarket circular, writing a note to a friend, writing a list of things to do, and reading a menu at a restaurant.

*Knowledge of narrative structure* involves understanding the nature of stories and how they are constructed. Knowledge of the structure of stories is important because most of the material used to teach reading to young children is written in narrative form. Children are likely to understand material presented in a form with which they are familiar. Reading and rereading storybooks aloud to children is one of the best ways to build a sense of stories. Storytelling by adults and children is entertaining and is a natural way to reinforce and extend children's conceptions of how characters, plot, setting, and other story elements work together to form narratives.

*Literacy as a source of enjoyment* refers to the development of a positive attitude toward reading and other literacy experiences. Children who have positive attitudes and expectations about reading are more likely to be motivated to learn to read. Adults can share books of all types: stories, informational books, and poetry. This is one of the best ways to promote a sense that reading is fun. Books that contain humor and language play provide enjoyment while fostering a sensitivity to language. Anyone who reads the title is not surprised that Joseph Slate's alliterative rhyming animal alphabet story, *Miss Bindergarten Gets Ready for Kindergarten* is a big hit with young children. Having paper, writing instruments, and books available for children's pretend play and independent exploration allows them to explore these materials on their own terms. Drawing and writing often become an integral part of pretending as children explore their use for self–expression.

> **I**t seems that opportunities to engage in extended discourse in the home build skills in producing extended discourse of precisely the type that is needed for high levels of literacy. (Snow & Tabors, 1996, pp. 76–77)

*Extending vocabulary and language patterns* involves the development of vocabulary and linguistic patterns children need to make good predictions about print. This book emphasizes the idea that making sense of print requires the use of a combination of semantic, syntactic, and graphophonic cues along with background knowledge. Children who have an abundance of opportunities to expand their language and linguistic repertoires are more apt to recognize words unknown to them as readers and to make sense of what they read. Participation in read–aloud activities in family and school situations, and in interesting talk at school and at the family dinner table appear to have a major influence on children's language abilities and their background knowledge.

## Strategies That Support Learning the Alphabet

Although children's ability to recognize the letters of the alphabet is an excellent predictor of first– and second–grade reading achievement, this knowledge probably reflects more about a child's general knowledge about books and print than the fact that he or she can name letters. In fact, children do not need to know all of the letters of the alphabet or know them in any particular order before they begin learning to read and write. The best practice is to help children identify letters and numbers in an enjoyable way as they acquire the broader concepts about print and books they will need as a foundation for literacy. The following are some tips for doing this:

- Focus on letters that have special meaning for children, such as the letters in their own names. This is more effective than simply teaching one arbitrary letter per week.

- Teach the alphabet song. This is fun for children and it gives them something to rely on when they attempt to use simple dictionaries or try to locate particular letters on alphabet charts.

- Post children's names in places that will help them identify them. Occasionally point to the letters, spelling their names for them.

- Print each letter of a child's name on separate cards or pieces of paper. Scramble them and let the child reconstruct his or her name as he or she matches the cut up version to a complete one.

- Read alphabet books on a regular basis and make them available for children to browse through on their own. Encourage children to work with a buddy and read together.

- Encourage children to experiment with letter forms. Use clay, finger paint, chalk and chalkboard, felt and sandpaper letters, alphabet puzzles, and wood and magnetic letters.

- Keep alphabet charts at children's eye level so that they can be referred to easily.

- Place children's names on index cards or place them in a pocket chart so that they can be removed and read closely. Use only a few names at a time. Ask children to locate their own names, find the names that start with the same letter or end with the same letter, and identify a particular letter that you display.

- Make simple picture dictionaries available.

- Help children make a class alphabet book or an in-dividual alphabet book.

## Strategies That Support Phonemic Awareness

Activities promoting phonemic awareness help children perceive their language as a series of sounds that they can pay attention to, segment, and categorize. Activities should be playful and game–like, much like the way children manipulate the language of songs, chants, and rhymes on their own. Keep the atmosphere informal and avoid putting children under any stress, which might make them retreat from participating and thus do more harm than good. Here are some ideas:

- Include nursery rhymes, poems, and storybooks with patterned rhymes in your daily read–aloud repertoire.
- Read poetry and stories that contain alliteration and word play, including alphabet books.
- When reading or chanting a familiar poem or rhyme, pause before a rhyming word and let children fill in the rhyme.
- Create your own simple rhymes and invite children to try some as well.
- Encourage and praise children's self–initiated attempts to memorize very simple rhymes and songs.
- When children are familiar with the concept of rhyme, make or purchase games that feature rhyming words. Children may match pictures that rhyme or they may use a bingo–type game board to cover pictures that rhyme with one drawn from the box.
- Invite children to clap the number of syllables they hear in someone's name. First say the name, then repeat it with the children as they clap with you; John

gets one clap, Mary gets two, Jonathan gets three, and so on.

- Help children to identify similarities in sounds. Model the following in a "sing–song" manner:

> *Ball* is a word that starts like *boy*.
> *Boy/ball; boy/ball.*
> Can you think of a word that starts like *boy*?

When a child responds correctly (for example, *Bill*) repeat:

> *Bill* is a word that starts like *boy*.
> *boy/Bill, boy/Bill.*
> Can you think of a word that starts like *boy*?

Encourage children to join subsequent rounds. After they grasp the idea, consider moving on to medial and final sounds. Keep the words simple and stress the sound clearly as well as its placement in the word (beginning, medial, or end).

- After children have a sense of what it means to attend to component sounds in words, invite them to try the following: Slowly stretch the sounds of short words with two or three sounds, such as *see* (2), *cat* (3), or *dish* (3). As you say each word, push a penny, small tile, or blank card forward for each sound heard: /c/ is one sound; /a/ is two; /t/ is three. Model this several times before you ask children to try it. Encourage children to use this stretching technique when they are attempting to spell words on their own.

# Strategies That Support Phonics

All of the activities recommended in support of phonemic awareness also relate directly to phonics. On the following page are some other recommendations.

- Take advantage of opportunities to discuss interesting sound–letter patterns in literature that you are reading aloud. Keep in mind that during the first or second reading of a book or story, it is best to respond to the content. That is, discuss the plot, characters, and ideas for information and enjoyment. After that, you may want to ask children if they have noticed anything special about certain words. Help them to establish the relations among words or parts of words that look and sound alike. Encourage this kind of "noticing" of written language in reading and writing activities throughout the day.

- Invite children to watch as you write messages and lists. Think aloud as you model the use of phonics to help with spelling. For example: "We need to make a list of the things we need to plant our seeds." Emphasizing the /d/, say, "*dirt* starts just like *dog*. I need to start with a *d*." You will not do this with every word or letter, but do enough so that children get the idea of how writers think when they spell. As children become knowledgeable about phonics, call on them to help when you think aloud. Let them tell the part they know as you fill in the rest.

- Use children's names to point out similarities and differences in the way they look and sound. Choose pairs such as *Jamal* and *Jennifer*. Have children notice how they look and sound alike at the beginning, middle, and end.

- Encourage children's attempts to write. Most often, the writing gradually moves from scribbling and forming strings of letters to an attempt to represent sounds with letters. When this occurs, encourage children to stretch the word, thinking about the way it sounds and the letter(s) that come to mind. Some children aim for "correctness" from the beginning. Give help, but let them know how much you value their own attempts. Encourage children to write the part they do know and leave the rest for your help later. Writing the sounds they hear helps children inter-nalize phonics. Make special attempts to acknowledge a child's "thoughtful" reasoning when his or her attempts appear logical to the child but produce unconventional spellings. For exam-ple, it would seem logical to begin the word *city* with an *s* or *truck* with *chr* at the beginning (Most young children pronounce it this way). As young chil-dren sort through these things, they need to know that their attempts are valued and show their ability as thinkers.

- When a child inquires about a word, use the opportunity to point out sound–letter relationships: "This one begins with *s*. It says *salt*. This one be-gins with *p* and says *pepper*."

- As you listen to children read, avoid immediately telling them words they do not know or read incorrectly. You might ask them to think about what makes sense and then look at the word together to sound it out. Help children divide words into man-ageable chunks rather than sounding out words letter by letter.

- Involve children in word–making activities (Cunning-ham & Cunningham, 1992) in which children are guided in creating words from letters they are given. During this 15–minute activity, children make 12 to 15 words, beginning with two–letter words and contin-uing with three–, four–, five–letter, and longer words until the final word is made. The final word (a six–,

> The teacher's job is to find out what understandings a particular child has and to use whatever materials or instruction can best help that child, and not be rigidly doctrinaire about his or her methods.... Some children have lots of content but desperately need help with form; others need content; still others, form and content. (Juel, 1993, p.135)

seven–, or eight–letter word) always includes all the letters they have that day. For example, from the word *spider*, children are guided in making the words *Ed*, *red*, *rid*, *sip*, *pie*, *pies*, *dies*, *side*, *ride*, *ripe*, *rise*, *pride*, and *drips*. Start by allowing children to work in small groups or pairs. Give constant feedback.

• Involve children in various sorting activities. Play games that require them to sort pictures into categories according to their beginning, medial, or ending sounds. Word sorting involves categorizing words with the same rhyming families, vowel generalizations, or other language pattern under study. Children enjoy manipulating picture cards and word cards. In contrast to worksheets, sorting involves children with a large number of examples and requires them to think analytically and critically. Simply adjust the level of the activity to the children's level of development (Bear, Invernizzi, Templeton, & Johnston, 1996).

• Develop a strategy of predicting, using multiple cueing systems. Using a familiar selection, choose a word and cover it with your finger or a piece of paper. Or, simply write a sentence, covering one word. Ask children to predict what words might fit in the empty slot. Write down each word as it is given. If a child offers a word that does not make sense, discuss it. At this point they are using semantic and syntactic cues. Uncover the first letter of the word. With the children's help, go through the list, eliminating each word that will not fit now that they have more information. Now, they have added phonics to the decoding cues they are using. Finally, uncover the whole word and examine it with the children to confirm or correct their predictions. Here is an example:

Bill likes to eat (pizza).
The children offer: hot dogs, ice cream, hamburgers, steak.
The teacher lists the words given.

The first letter is uncovered and it is the letter *p*.

The children go through the list, only to discover that none of the words will fit.

They list new words. Now they should only give words beginning with the letter *p*.

The word is uncovered so that they can confirm or correct their predictions.

(Note: If the word begins with a consonant blend, uncover the blend rather than just the first consonant.)

# Strategies That Support Onset-Rime Analogies

Keep in mind that the analogy strategy is limited by the knowledge of onsets and rimes learners have stored in their memory. For example, a learner who does not have the word *can* stored in his or her memory will be unable to use the analogy strategy to identify *pan*. Obviously, the greater the number of words with varied rimes learners have in their reading vocabularies, the more useful the analogy strategy. Wylie and Durrell (1970) identified 37 phonograms that could be found in almost 500 primary-grade words. These high-utility phonograms are: *ack, ail, ain, ake, ale, ame, an, ank, ap, ash, at, ate, aw, ay, eat, ell, est, ice, ick, ide, ight, ill, in, ine, ing, ink, ip, it, ock, oke, op, ore, ot, uck, ug, ump,* and *unk*. This is a useful list for generating activities. Some suggested activities follow:

- Play simple consonant-substitution games: Start with a known word such as *cat*. Using the chalkboard, demonstrate what happens when the *c* in *cat* is substituted for other consonants. You might find it helpful to chant the following in a sing-song manner:

  You take the c away from *cat*, put in *p* and you get *pat*.
  You take the p away from *pat*, put in *f* and you get *fat*.

Continue in this manner, making as many words as you can that children are likely to have in their listening vocabularies. After the children have caught on, pause before saying the new word and see if they can identify it. Continue doing the same with other known words with high–utility phonograms.

> **O**ur vision of an ideal classroom, one consistent with the types of classrooms excellent teachers have been telling us about in our research, includes authentic reading and writing as well as opportunities to hone the skills that comprise reading and writing, with all of the educational opportunities doled out in doses appropriate to the needs of particular students. (Pressley, 1994, p. 166)

- Using a known word, have students generate as many words as they can that rhyme with it. Write down each word. Guide children to notice the similarities. For example: Here is the word *ride*. Can you think of some words that rhyme with *ride*? When a rhyming word does not conform to the spelling pattern, simply write it down. Guide children to notice the difference. Then move that word into another column to show that it gets sorted differently.

- Play "I Am Thinking of a Word." It begins like *ball* and rhymes with *tack*. What could it be? Have children guess orally first. After they have caught on, have them write the word independently and then share what they have written. Remember to stick to words that are within the children's listening vocabularies. Using nonsense words or words with which they are unfamiliar may confuse children, rather than help them link these activities to real reading.

- Guide children to use onset–rime analogies with other word identification strategies linked to meaning. Write a sentence on the board, such as, *Mother put the _____ on the table*. It begins like *dog* and rhymes with *wish*. What could it be?

- The following activity is designed for learners who have experienced difficulty in their initial attempt at learning to read. Involve children in word-study activities in which they work closely with words, segmenting them, analyzing them, and discussing them. This kind of activity not only makes the patterns in language visible, it helps children store the fully analyzed words into their memories for use in forming analogies. Gaskins et al. (1996–1997) suggested that teachers model and provide guided practice in self-talk strategies similar to the one following, which was designed to help students learn words containing rimes for use with onset–rime analogies:

The teacher begins by giving the word orally. This makes it easier for students to focus on the sounds:

1. The word is _____.
2. Stretch the word. I hear _____ sounds.

Students are shown the word and it is analyzed in terms of what students already know about language patterns. For example:

3. I see _____ letters because _____.
4. The spelling pattern is _____.
5. This is what I know about the vowel: _____.
6. A word that rhymes with this one is _____.

Or, another word on the word wall* with the same vowel sound is _____.

Learning to read is not something that begins in Grade 1 or starts with memorizing the alphabet. From infancy, children are emerging as literate human beings. Virtually

---

*The word wall consists of a list of key words that are high-frequency words in English and have common spelling patterns. The words are posted for all to view.

everything they learn about language and about their world contributes to their becoming literate. The everyday activities during which children observe adults using print to accomplish tasks and in which children involve literacy in their play are among the most powerful literacy lessons a child can have. Sharing books and engaging in interesting conversations with responsive adults provide the foundation for children's interest in learning to read. These experiences stimulate children's curiosity and inform and motivate their personal explorations with print.

Teachers can select from a wide variety of instructional activities to promote students' phonemic awareness, knowledge and use of phonics, and use of onset–rime analogies for reading and writing. In selecting activities, teachers must be mindful of the age and developmental levels of students, the need to keep instruction engaging for young learners, and the need to create a context that allows children to make connections between the activities in which they are engaged and their use in meaningful literacy acts.

# CHAPTER 6

# Shaping Curriculum: Instruction and Assessment

igh standards for student achievement have become the basis for reform at national, state, and local levels. A broadly stated standard such as "Students will read and respond effectively to a variety of types of texts" is intended as a general guideline for educators K–12. However, the statement must be expanded on to provide a framework for instruction at specific grade levels. In the case of word identification, teachers of beginning reading want to know what students should know and be able to do in order to meet the standard. School districts have a responsibility to make it clear to teachers what is expected of them and their students at various grade levels or grade-level groupings (for example, primary) relative to the standards they have adopted. Curriculum frameworks should be linked to the standards and should include a delineation of the specific objectives involved, suggested instructional strategies, and suggested strategies for ongoing assessment. Staff development is critical to ensuring that the curriculum frameworks are addressed in a manner that reflects a school district's philosophy and intent.

## Curriculum Frameworks for Decoding Instruction (K–2)

Figures 15, 16, and 17 offer examples of curriculum frameworks for teaching word identification strategies,

## Figure 15  Kindergarten Curriculum Framework

*Typical state standard for reading*
**Students apply a wide range of strategies to comprehend, interpret, evaluate, and appreciate texts.**

*Typical district grade-level application (decoding only)—Kindergarten level*
Students have knowledge and use of the following:

> Directionality—left page before right, top to bottom, and left to right line of print and return sweep;
>
> Visual matching—short sentences, phrases, words, and letters;
>
> Locating known words—letters in familiar text, high-frequency phrases and words;
>
> Alphabet knowledge—identify and match most upper- and lower-case letters;
>
> Phonemic awareness—hears separate words in sentences and syllables in words; matches like sounds in words (beginning and end), and recognizes rhyming words;
>
> Phonics—alphabetic principle (awareness); knowledge of some initial consonant sound–letter relationships;
>
> Small sight vocabulary—recognizes own name; some high-frequency environmental print; and
>
> Independent practice—makes use of opportunities to read and write independently.

**Instructional strategies**
• Read aloud to children from a wide variety of materials.
• Involve children in a variety of shared reading and writing activities.
• Involve children in varied reader response activities (art, drama, writing, etc.).
• Involve children in activities designed to help them use the conventions of written language: directionality, concept of a word, and the language of literacy.
• Involve children in activities designed to promote phonemic awareness, awareness of alphabetic principle, and some sound–letter correspondences.
• Involve children in activities designed to help them visually match sentences, words, letters (upper/lower case), and other symbols.
• Involve children in activities designed to help them learn letter names.
• Provide time for independent reading.
• Make a wide variety of materials available.
• Provide opportunities for children to acquire a small sight vocabulary.
• Encourage children to engage in book activities outside the classroom.

*(continued)*

| Figure 15  Kindergarten Curriculum Framework (continued) |
| --- |

**Assessment strategies**
- Documented observations during whole- and small-group instruction (for example, anecdotal records, work samples).
- Assessment during one-to-one conferences (for example, anecdotal records, developmental checklists, and inventories).
- Monitoring system for at-home reading.
- Informal documentation of interest in books and attempts at independent reading.
- Documentation of independent writing (for example, work samples).

**Teachers are responsible for:**

**Evidence of regularly planned activities of the type listed under instructional strategies.**

**Current documentation for each child based on procedures listed under assessment strategies.**

including phonics, in Kindergarten and Grades 1 and 2. The idea is to give teachers clear guidance for instruction as well as ways to gather evidence about what children know and where they need help. Under the best circumstances, guidelines of this type would be developed cooperatively by teachers, administrators, and parents so that all involved would have a shared vision of what students should know and how they should perform at a particular level of instruction. In addition, there would be some agreement on the kinds of instructional strategies that are used and the assessment strategies in place to document progress. Teachers would be expected to show evidence of planning for these to occur. Benchmarks, outlining acceptable levels of performance also could be established. Note that in the examples given, the instructional strategies are similar for Grades 1 and 2. The key difference in these two grades is the use of increasingly difficult materials. Some differences will occur in the range of word recognition strategies covered at these two grade levels. (*Please note that these curriculum frameworks are not meant to be prescriptive, but to serve as guides for districts to develop their own frameworks for use by classroom teachers.*)

---

## Figure 16  Grade 1 Curriculum Framework

*Typical state standard for reading*
**Students apply a wide range of strategies to comprehend, interpret, evaluate, and appreciate texts.**

*Typical district grade level application (decoding only)—Grade 1 (Also see kindergarten list)*

Students demonstrate knowledge and use of the following:

Onset–rime analogies—uses patterns in known words to identify unfamiliar words;

Phonemic awareness—matches similar medial sounds in short words; segments and blends phonemes in short words;

Phonics—initial and final consonants, medial consonants, initial consonant clusters, initial and final consonant digraphs, and short and long vowels and some vowel generalizations;

Structural analysis—compound words; some contractions; common inflectional endings;

Multiple cueing systems for word recognition—semantics (word meaning), syntax (grammatical structure), and graphophonic (sounds–letters);

Cross checking (one cue against another);

Self-correction strategies to preserve meaning;

Sight vocabulary of high-frequency words and interesting words;

Independent practice—Makes use of opportunities to read and write independently.

(continued)

---

## Figure 16  Grade 1 Curriculum Framework (continued)

**Instructional strategies**

Apply strategies at increasingly difficult levels:

• Read aloud to children from a wide variety of materials—narratives, expository, and poetry.
• Involve children in shared reading activities.
• Involve children in varied reader–response activities, including writing.
• Involve children in activities designed to help them use graphophonic, semantic, and syntactic cues for reading.
• Involve children in activities designed specifically to promote the use of phonics in reading and spelling.
• Involve children in activities designed to help them segment language.
• Involve children in activities designed to help them use their background knowledge to make sense of what they are reading.
• Involve children in activities designed to help them learn to use the conventions of written language to make sense of what they are reading.
• Provide time for daily independent reading.
• Make a wide variety of materials available, including technology.
• Involve children in high–frequency vocabulary activities connected to meaningful content.
• Involve children in rereading activities to develop fluency.
• Involve children in an ongoing home reading program.

**Assessment**

• Documented observations during whole– and small–group instruction (for example, anecdotal records or work samples).
• Assessment during one–to–one conferences (for example, running records, developmental checklists, and inventories).
• Monitoring system for at–home reading.
• Documentation of independent reading (book lists).
• Documentation of independent writing (analysis of work samples).

**Teachers are responsible for:**

**Evidence of regularly planned activities of the type listed under instructional strategies.**

**Current documentation for each child based on procedures listed under assessment strategies.**

# Monitoring Progress

Shared and guided reading and writing most often are group experiences. As group activities, they lend themselves to an overall assessment of the students involved. However, group activities also can provide a window into the development of individuals. Because of behavior exhibited during a group activity, a student may be selected for special

---

## Figure 17  Grade 2 Curriculum Framework

*Typical state standard for reading*
**Students apply a wide range of strategies to comprehend, interpret, evaluate, and appreciate texts.**

*Typical district grade level application (decoding only)—Grade 2 (Also see Grade 1 list)*

Students demonstrate knowledge and use of the following:

Multiple cueing systems for word recognition—semantics (word meaning), syntax (grammatical structure), and graphophonic (sounds–letters);

Cross checking (one cue against another);

Self-correction strategies to preserve meaning;

Phonemic awareness—increasing ability to segment words for phonics/spelling;

Onset–rime analogies—increasing ability to use patterns in known words to identify unknown words;

Phonics—increasing ability to use knowledge of short, long, and some vowel generalizations; consonant clusters and digraphs (initial and final; two and three letter); hard and soft *g*, and others to be determined by the teacher;

Structural analysis—increasingly difficult root/base words, prefixes, suffixes, compound words, contractions, and common inflectional endings;

Independent practice—makes use of opportunities to read and write material of increasing difficulty independently; and

Sight vocabulary of high frequency words is expanded.

*(continued)*

---

## Figure 17  Grade 2 Curriculum Framework (continued)

**Instructional strategies**

Apply strategies at increasingly difficult levels:

- Read aloud to children from a wide variety of materials—narratives, expository, and poetry.
- Involve children in shared reading activities.
- Involve children in varied reader–response activities, including writing.
- Involve children in activities designed to help them use graphophonic, semantic, and syntactic cues for reading.
- Involve children in activities designed specifically to promote the use of phonics in reading and spelling.
- Involve children in activities designed to help them segment language.
- Involve children in activities designed to help them use their background knowledge to make sense of what they are reading.
- Involve children in activities designed to help them learn to use the conventions of written language to make sense of what they are reading.
- Provide time for daily independent reading.
- Make a wide variety of materials available, including technology.
- Involve children in a variety of vocabulary activities connected to meaningful content.
- Involve children in a rereading activities to develop fluency.
- Involve children in an ongoing home reading program.

**Assessment**

- Documented observations during whole- and small–group instruction (for example, anecdotal records, and work samples).
- Assessment during one–to–one conferences (for example, running records, developmental checklists, and inventories).
- Monitoring system for at–home reading.
- Documentation of independent reading (for example, list of books read).
- Documentation of independent writing (for example, analysis of independent writing.

**Teachers are responsible for:**

**Evidence of regularly planned activities of the type listed under instructional strategies.**

**Current documentation for each child based on procedures listed under assessment strategies.**

monitoring. For example, a child may rarely participate in the group. In this case, there is a need to determine whether or not this is due to low ability, shyness, health factors (such as vision or hearing problems), or other reasons. Or, a child may appear to be functioning at a very advanced level, and closer observations can help determine whether or not this child is ready for more challenging materials.

*Checklists* offer a guide to the instructional components that might be addressed and monitored during instruction. Each school district is likely to construct its own set of guidelines, which should be made available for parents if they wish to examine them. Figure 18 is a detailed list of items usually included on checklists for emergent literacy and beginning reading programs. Keep in mind that the list focuses on strategies designed primarily to promote word recognition. It can be helpful for teachers who wish to construct their own checklists for the analysis of work samples and for assessment. Every district should have a literacy curriculum in place that goes beyond this list to include strategies specific to reading comprehension, literary analysis, and written composition at the beginning reading level. Checklists of the type shown in Figure 19 on pages 76–77 are typical of tools used for recording and assessing the observations of children's progress.

*Anecdotal records* taken during and after group work or one–to–one conferences can provide direction for decision making about future learning experiences. Some teachers use a clipboard and labels to quickly write down their thoughts. These are later placed in the teacher's planbook or in a child's folder. Figure 20 on page 77 shows some anecdotal notes written by a first–grade teacher, who has made a special effort to track a child's behavior during group writing activities.

*Work samples* can provide insight into how well a group and the individuals within a group are progressing. When these are produced under the teacher's close direction, immediate feedback is given to problems associated with both

# Figure 18  Assessing Young Children's Emerging Literacy Development

Observing children's literacy behavior on an informal basis is one of the best ways to determine how a child is progressing. The work of Marie Clay (1989) provides the basis for most checklists of emerging literacy. The checklists serve as an assessment for teachers as well. These skills and demonstrations of understanding cannot be observed unless we provide the environment for them to occur. *Keep in mind that the concepts related to emerging literacy are best learned through daily experiences with print and books and not through drill.*

## Concepts about books and print

The child demonstrates an understanding and use of:

_____ Directionality of reading material:

            _____ right side up _____ front to back

            _____ left to right    _____ top to bottom

_____ Title        _____ Author        _____ Illustrator

_____ Print as a source of meaning and language

_____ Pictures as sources of meaning

_____ Words/wordness: _____ as composed of letters _____ as matched to speech

            _____ spaces between words

_____ Language to talk about literacy: word, letter, book, story, poem, page, line, title, author, illustrator, beginning, end, and so on.

## Interest in books, reading, and writing

The child:

_____ shows an interest in listening to stories read aloud.

_____ participates in reading patterned and predictable language.

_____ engages in talk about books; recalls important parts and information in the stories.

_____ requests favorite books, such as nursery rhymes.

_____ chooses to look at books as an independent activity.

_____ views himself/herself as a reader.

_____ makes attempts at writing (in whatever way he or she can) and reads what was written.

_____ shows an awareness of the many purposes for reading and writing.

_____ shows an increasing curiosity about the world and a growing understanding and willingness to talk about new concepts and ideas.

## Figure 19  Assessing Knowledge and Use of Word Recognition Strategies for Beginning Reading

**Attention to components and patterns in the language:**
**Foundational strategies**
Note: These strategies usually are included in the kindergarten and early first–grade curriculum. They are taught through a balance of direct and indirect instruction. This list does not focus specifically on strategies for reading comprehension, literary analysis, or written composition. The child:

_____ infers, orally, words in cloze–type activities (he or she fills in the acceptable word when the adult pauses during oral reading).

_____ matches, visually, repeated words, and phrases.

_____ recognizes own name and its individual letters.

_____ recognizes increasing number of letters other than those in his or her own name

_____ tracks print accurately with hand or finger.

_____ notices similarities in words and letters.

_____ recognizes when words rhyme.

_____ hears number of syllables.

_____ has small, but increasing and stable, sight vocabulary.

**Attention to components and patterns in the language:**
**Phonics and word analysis**
Note: These generally are included in the first–grade curriculum over the course of an entire year.
The child demonstrates knowledge and use of the following:

_____ initial and final consonants

_____ short and long vowels

_____ initial consonant blends

_____ initial consonant digraphs

_____ some vowel generalizations (cvc, cvvc, cvc+e )

_____ onset–rime analogies

_____ compound words

_____ inflectional endings (–ing, –ed)

_____ plurals with *s*

_____ contractions

*(continued)*

## Figure 19  Assessing Knowledge and Use of Word Recognition Strategies for Beginning Reading (continued)

**Observations During Oral Reading**

The child:

_____ reads with appropriate expression.

_____ self–corrects to preserve meaning.

_____ observes punctuation to construct meaning.

_____ takes risks in pronunciation of unfamiliar words when reading new materials.

_____ is strategic when confronting unfamiliar words. For example,

- skips the word and continues to read for more information;
- rereads the sentence;
- uses context clues;
- uses picture clues;
- uses knowledge of familiar words and word parts (analogies); or
- attempts to sound out the word.

**Observations During Writing**

The child:

_____ applies phonics and word–analysis strategies in attempting to spell.

_____ uses spaces between words.

_____ takes risks in attempting to spell.

_____ writes some words using conventional spelling.

_____ shows development in the use of capitalization:
Uses I at the beginning of sentences; capitalizes names of people and places.

_____ shows development in the use of punctuation.

## Figure 20  Anecdotal Notes

9/15 Byron does not participate in shared writing, but seems attentive.

9/29 B offered the *b* to begin the word *bird*—a start.

10/10 B seems to have caught on to what sound and symbols are all about.

Contributed several times during group writing.

teaching and learning. When similar problems occur across a large number of students, it signals the teacher to stop the lesson and revisit the material under study. Work samples acquired through independent work are excellent sources of information because they let the teacher know how well a child is able to apply known strategies to new situations. Samples of written material composed by the child and assessments of oral reading from new material on the child's instructional level offer the most useful information (see the first–grade work sample in Figure 21). Again, teachers try to determine how well a child is doing in relationship to the

## Figure 21  Work Sample–Grade 1

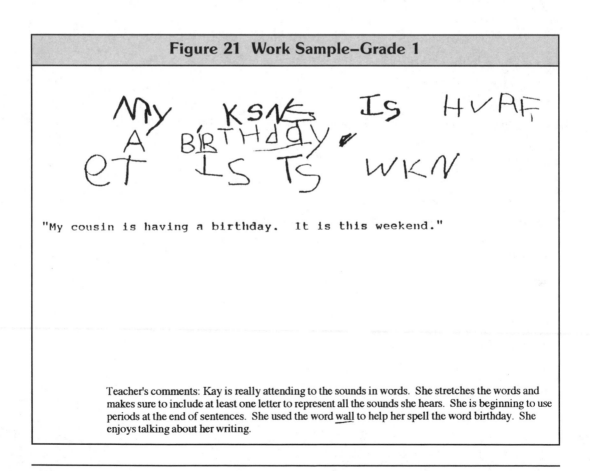

"My cousin is having a birthday.  It is this weekend."

Teacher's comments: Kay is really attending to the sounds in words. She stretches the words and makes sure to include at least one letter to represent all the sounds she hears. She is beginning to use periods at the end of sentences. She used the word wall to help her spell the word birthday. She enjoys talking about her writing.

## Figure 22  Reading At Home

TO: At–Home Reading Buddy

FROM: _____ Mrs. Roades _____

Please read the enclosed book with your reading buddy. Do at least one activity, fill out the form, and return it tomorrow. Thank you.

(Name of child) _____ Sammy Clayton _____and I

read (Name of book) _____ Hop On Frog _____together.

We also... (briefly tell what else you did) – _____ We talked about the

story and Sammy drew a picture of the frog. _____

Following are some suggested activities that can be done with any book:

Discuss the story.                          Read the story again with another reading
                                            buddy.
Draw a picture to go with the book          Tape record a second reading at home.
Write another story like this one.          Make a puppet of one of the story
                                            characters.
Act out parts of the story.                 Write about your favorite part .

Bill Clayton _____ Date ___ Jan. 24 ___
(signed by Reading Buddy at home)

## Figure 23  Read-At-Home Log

| Book Title | Student's Name or Initials |
| --- | --- |
|  |  |
|  |  |
|  |  |
|  |  |
|  |  |

group and in relationship to himself or herself over time, and try to identify the problems that seem to persist across the group that indicate a need for whole–group or small–group attention.

## Monitoring At-Home and Independent Reading

A planned program for independent reading is indispensable. Time for reading self–selected books in school and a system for sharing books at home offers the child more time on task. It also involves the home in a way that makes it an active part of the process and offers an opportunity to monitor the child's development over time. Developing a simple but focused system for the use of materials at home lets everyone involved know how important an independent reading program is. The at–home reading buddy may be a parent, an older sibling, or any interested person who is willing to help. Figure 22 on page 79 shows a Reading–At–Home form that can be duplicated and sent home in a plastic bag along with the book. The Read–At–Home Log in Figure 23 can be completed at school by the child. A form such as this may be used for independent reading at school as well.

Teachers have an important influence on how much time children spend reading independently both during school and after school hours. Those who are successful in increasing home reading practice for their students have a deliberate plan in place and make it a high priority. They consistently supply appropriate books, have a system for monitoring home reading experiences, and encourage both children and their home partners to make reading a priority.

# CHAPTER 7

# Articulating the Phonics Program to Parents and the Community

In my travels around the country, I have the good fortune to speak to parents, school–board members, and educators. It will come as no surprise that there is great apprehension over the public perception that schools are not as good as they used to be—especially when it comes to teaching basic skills. Following are some of the questions that I am most frequently asked, followed by my responses in which I speak directly to the parent or caregiver. I hope that these will prove useful as points of discussion.

**Why don't they teach phonics anymore?** The teaching of phonics never has been abandoned. However, it is likely to look different today than it did when you were in school. Today's young children are just as likely to learn phonics through their writing as they are through their reading. Emphasis is placed on using phonics in conjunction with other word recognition strategies. Nevertheless, you may have good reason to question whether or not your child is receiving enough instruction in word recognition. Speak to your child's teacher and ask him or her to explain how phonics is addressed in the reading and writing program.

**Is there a certain amount of phonics that all children should have?** No. The term phonics really refers to *instruction* in sound–letter relationships. Because some children figure out these relations with very little instruction, it is foolish to waste their time with something that is meant to help them do what they already know how to do. On the other hand, some children do need extensive help with phonics. In most classrooms, teachers provide a relatively standard curriculum for all students, which is modified to meet the varied needs of individuals. They do this by observing children's attempts as they read and spell. Based on these observations, teachers work with individuals and small groups to provide additional help.

**How will I know whether or not my child is receiving enough phonics instruction or when there is a reading problem?** First, it is important to realize that you will be unable to tell how much phonics a child is receiving by the number of worksheets and workbook pages he or she brings home. Because today's teachers are more likely to teach phonics in a way that requires them to apply it directly to their reading and writing, rather than as an isolated exercise, children will receive instruction in conjunction with reading and writing of real texts, such as books, stories, and charts. Practice of these skills and strategies will involve more work with real texts rather than skills sheets. You do have important windows through which you can observe your child's use of phonics, however. One is by observing your child's reading errors during oral reading. The other is by observing your child's spelling attempts during writing. You probably have some idea of what should be expected. Nevertheless, you might want to note the kinds of errors you observe and consult with your child's teacher as to whether or not these are things he or she should be expected to know. Keep in mind that all mistakes are not equal. At times, when your child gives a word other than the one written on the page, you may want to ask "What made you say that?" You may find that the problem involves something other than phonics. Equally important, you may gain some insight as to how your child attempts to make sense of written material.

**Should phonics instruction continue throughout the grades?**  Phonics instruction should be concentrated in the first few grades. Alternative strategies and special instructional programs may need to be provided for children who have had the benefit of a sound phonics program and who still are experiencing difficulty learning to read and write. Instruction in structural analysis, which often is confused with phonics, continues throughout the grades.

**Is it possible for a child to have too much phonics?**  Yes; children who demonstrate the ability to apply phonics successfully in conjunction with other word recognition strategies should spend their time on challenging reading and writing activities, rather than the phonics activities designed

*A student reinforcing letter recognition.*

for the whole class. Some children may have been taught phonics at the expense of other word recognition strategies, leaving them with an over–reliance on one method of word recognition. These children are likely to become stuck, with no alternative word recognition strategies, when they see words for which phonics alone will not work. These children need a better balance of word identification strategies and need help with the ability to cross check and self–correct during the use of those strategies.

**When teachers allow children to invent spelling, isn't that teaching incorrect spelling?** No; children are aware that their temporary spellings do not conform to adult standards. They understand that their attempts only approximate what is conventional, just as a baby's first steps and early speech only approximate adult behavior. Allowing children to apply what they know about phonics to help them spell is an important first step in helping them become independent writers, and it frees them to communicate their ideas. They realize that their spelling will change with increasing experience with written language and continued instruction.

**At what age should children be expected to learn correct spelling?** As with all aspects of literacy, spelling is developmental. Children will progress at different rates. Teachers track the spelling development of their students. They observe which aspects of children's spelling adhere to standard forms and which do not, intervening with group and individual instruction when appropriate. Keep in mind that children will continue to experiment with new words and spelling patterns as they need them in their writing. For example, a teacher may be quite satisfied with the spelling of the word *wrinkle* as *rinkl*, realizing that neither the silent *w* in *wr* or the final *le* is something that has been covered instructionally and that *wrinkle* is not a word this child would be expected to have in his or her visual memory. Yet, it was obviously an important word for this child to include in his or her story. Teachers make a distinction between what a child should and should not be held accountable for.

**Is there a point when invented spelling should stop?** Again, if we assume that instruction is continuing through-out the grades and children are held accountable for what has been taught, then it follows naturally that a student's spelling should become less and less unconventional. By third grade or so, teachers begin to look at specific patterns of error within a child's spelling and address those needs more specifically. Most teachers agree that there seem to be some issues that need constant revisiting, such as the homophones *there* and *their*. Some spelling generalizations and some aspects of word study such as Latin and Greek roots generally are not addressed during the primary grades.

**What should I look for in my school's beginning literacy program?** Even within the same district, schools can differ widely in their approach to literacy. Within the same school, teachers may vary in their overall approach, even when they use the same materials. Nevertheless, you can get a sense of the overall stance or vision of a school by asking the teacher and principal a few questions in a direct, non-threatening manner. Remember, even when the answers are not what you expected, you might want to take a "wait and see" approach and then express your concerns. More than likely you will want to ask questions and observe in class-rooms to determine some of the following:

*The school's general orientation toward literacy instruction.* Administrators and teachers should be able to ex-plain, in simple terms, how they approach literacy instruc-tion in general as well as how they address phonics. Beware, if they merely say they use the XYZ program. Although you might want to see those materials, they should really be a reflection of the district's and teacher's philosophical stance and curriculum goals. Materials alone should not drive the curriculum. If you are especially worried about phonics and spelling, ask for one or two specific examples of how it is taught and how your child's progress will be monitored.

***The curriculum goals for the grade level(s) you are most interested in.*** Teachers should be able to give you a clear idea of what generally is expected of most children by the end of the year in the particular grade they teach. This may be included in a curriculum guide or in a parent booklet of some sort, he or she may orally share some general information about grade–level curriculum goals.

***The library facilities.*** Young children need plenty of opportunities and encouragement to practice the skills they are learning. Access to an abundance of interesting materials makes this practice possible. It is no wonder that virtually everyone agrees that a school's library collection is the backbone of literacy instruction. You should inquire about the classroom library and school library facilities. You also will want to know if a professional librarian is available to work with teachers and students and how much access children have to books on a daily basis.

***Evidence of differentiated instruction.*** Differentiating instruction to meet individual learner needs is perhaps the most important and challenging thing that teachers do. Is there evidence that the teacher varies instruction to include whole–group, small–group, and some personalized activities? Teachers who do this are more likely to get to know your child well and adapt instruction accordingly.

***Provisions for children who are experiencing difficulty.*** Although it is good to know that there are support programs outside the regular classroom, it is equally important to know how the classroom teacher addresses the problems of the struggling students as well. Among the things you might expect are extra small–group instruction, extra one-to-one conferences, and the use of special materials.

***Provisions for children who are advanced in their literacy development.*** More than likely, any special provisions for the advanced beginning readers will be concentrated in the classroom. You will want to know about plans to provide more challenging tasks and materials for these children.

***The classroom procedures for monitoring progress.*** There should be evidence of some type of ongoing classroom assessment. You might expect the teacher to keep folders with work samples, such as children's independent writing. Records of notes or checklists completed during one–to–one conferences also may be included as well as lists of some of the books children have read independently. Beware if you simply are shown a report card rather than the evidence on which the report card grades are based, and be concerned if the folders are merely filled with skill sheets and workbook pages, rather than applications of skills in meaningful situations.

***The support for home and school connections.*** Ask about what the school expects from parents and caregivers in the home. What type of homework activities are expected? Is homework based merely on a particular number of minutes per night or is there an attempt to provide meaningful home activities that are linked to the school curriculum? Is there a procedure for monitoring homework? Are parent meetings and conferences scheduled that might help you get a sense of the school program?

**What can I do at home to help my child read and write?** Obviously, the activities you might do at home to encourage reading and writing are similar to those already listed in Chapter 5. Nevertheless, I will emphasize some that are particularly important as support from the home.

- Every topic listed in Chapter 5 is best developed at home in an informal risk–free environment. Print awareness, print concepts, the functions of print, a knowledge of narrative structure, and literacy as a source of enjoyment are the foundation on which phonemic awareness and phonics are built.

- Read to and with your child on a daily basis. When reading familiar books, encourage your child to read along. Pause occasionally and let your child fill in an obvious word. Talk about the content of books and relate the content to your shared experience and to other books.

- Read and reread favorite nursery rhymes. Sing favorite songs and rhymes, reinforcing the language patterns and rhyme.

- When your child begins to read independently, show him how proud you are of each new accomplishment.

- When your child comes to an unfamiliar word, wait before you interject an answer. He may be attempting to figure it out independently. After a while, you might ask what he thinks might make sense or how the word might sound.

- If your child is making a great number of errors, the book probably is too hard. Ask the teacher to suggest some easier material. If this is "required reading," read the book to the child first and then ask him to read it to you. Meanwhile, continue to read easier material to build confidence and allow your child to practice skills.

- Write with your child. Allow him to help with the spelling of words for grocery lists or family reminders to be posted on the refrigerator. Offer congratulations for his help with the parts of words he knows.

- Play simple word games: I am thinking of a word...
  It rhymes with play. (*day, say*)
  It tastes good on toast and it begins like *ball*. (*butter*)
  Accept any reasonable answer. After the child catches on, have him make up a riddle for you to guess.

- When your child attempts to write independently, first pay attention to the content—what he is trying to say. Then, praise him for the *parts* of words spelled correctly as well as those completely correct by conventional standards. Also praise any attempts that suggest progress beyond what has been introduced at school or that you would not expect him to know. You might make a comment about sound–letter relationships you think he should know and offer a reminder or some help. If he wishes to revise or edit his work, you can offer to help. Remember, it is important that children understand that you do not expect every word to be spelled conventionally. You *are* looking for overall progress toward conventional spelling, however.

Today's educators are acutely aware of the importance of good public relations, both with parents and with the broader community at large. A truly effective home–school communication program is one that anticipates the kinds of concerns that parents may have and launches a strong proactive effort to enlist parental and community support before major misunderstandings develop. In many cases, the questions and concerns parents raise are those they should not have to ask in the first place. Potentially misunderstood aspects of the curriculum should be well articulated through ongoing efforts such as parent conferences, workshops, and newsletters. Educators need the insight and energy of the most concerned parents as allies, not opponents. Both share the same goal—the best education for children.

# Phonics Quiz for Teachers

Throughout this book many phonics–related terms have been used. You may have only a vague recollection of them from your early years as a student learning to read. As a skilled reader yourself, you may wonder how on earth you learned to read without knowing all these terms. The truth is that you can be a highly accomplished reader without knowing very much *about* phonics. As you learned to read, you focused on the *use* of phonics and other word recognition strategies. Now as someone who has chosen to assist others in learning to read, you are taking time to step outside the reading process and think of it as an object to be analyzed and discussed. This requires knowing something about the various strategies that typically are taught as well as the labels for them. Knowledge about phonics will help you to evaluate and use instructional materials and curriculum guides. The following quiz is excerpted partly from *The Phonics Test for Teachers* (Durkin, 1964). You might like to try it with a friend. Discuss the reasons for your answers before you check the answer key on pages 94–95. *Remember, this is not offered as something to be used with children. It is offered as background information for those who wish to help children learn to read.*

# Phonics Quiz for Teachers

## Vowels: Long and Short

Very often, vowels record what are generally called "long" sounds and "short" sounds. Knowledge of both sounds, for each of the five vowels, is evaluated here.

A. In each of the five rows of words listed below, underline the one word that be–gins with a *long* vowel sound.

| | | |
|---|---|---|
| 1. all | ask | apron |
| 2. eager | early | edge |
| 3. ignore | idle | irrigate |
| 4. odd | ocean | order |
| 5. up | urge | use |

B. In each of the five rows of words listed below, underline the *one* word that begins with a *short* vowel sound.

| | | |
|---|---|---|
| 1. ace | all | at |
| 2. eagle | earn | engine |
| 3. ice | ill | irk |
| 4. octave | owl | over |
| 5. ugly | use | urgent |

## Vowel Generalizations

Certain factors within a word affect the sounds recorded by the vowels in that word. Knowledge of these factors is evaluated below.

Answer each section by checking the appropriate blank and by writing the relevant generalization.

A.                                                                                              a i f

1. If *aif* were a syllable in a word, the letter *a* in that syllable would probably:

_____ sound like the *a* in *ate*
_____ sound like the *a* in *ask*
_____ be silent

2. The letter *i* in that syllable would probably:

_____ sound like the *i* in *ice*
_____ sound like the *i* in *inch*
_____ be silent

Excerpted by permission of the publisher from Durkin, D., *Phonics Test for Teachers*, (New York: Teachers College Press, ©1964 by Teachers College, Columbia University. All rights reserved.).

*(continued)*

## Phonics Quiz for Teachers (continued)

3. Why would *a* and *i* most likely record these sounds?

B.                                                                           e k

   1. If *ek* were a syllable in a word, the
      letter *e* in that syllable would probably:

                                   \_\_\_\_\_ sound like the *e* in *eat*
                                   \_\_\_\_\_ sound like the *e* in *end*
                                   \_\_\_\_\_ be silent

   2. Why would the letter *e* most likely record this sound?

C.                                                                           b u

   1. If *bu* were a syllable in a word, the
      letter *u* in that syllable would probably:

                                   \_\_\_\_\_ sound like the *u* in *use*
                                   \_\_\_\_\_ sound like the *u* in *us*
                                   \_\_\_\_\_ be silent

2. Why would *us* most likely record this sound?

**Digraphs**

Certain combinations of consonants are called *digraphs*. Knowledge of the consonant digraphs and of the digraph sounds is evaluated here.

A. Define the term *consonant digraph:*

B. In the words listed randomly below, find the eight words that contain a consonant digraph. In each of these eight words, underline the two letters that make up the digraph.

| | | | |
|---|---|---|---|
| thief | stain | cough | dumb |
| chalet | phase | fish | write |
| crust | skip | try | there |
| sting | plane | rich | brown |

Excerpted by permission of the publisher from Durkin, D., *Phonics Test for Teachers*, (New York: Teachers College Press, ©1964 by Teachers College, Columbia University. All rights reserved.).

*(continued)*

### Consonant Blends

Certain combinations of consonants are called *consonant blends*. Knowledge of consonant blends is evaluated here.

A. Define the term consonant blend:

B. Find the eight words that contain a consonant blend. In each of these eight words underline the letters that make up the blend.

| | | | |
|---|---|---|---|
| blank | comb | shout | trap |
| kite | spring | twig | camel |
| grain | gasp | foam | gnaw |
| split | write | cane | rusty |

### Diphthongs

Certain combinations of vowels are called diphthongs. At times, the consonants y and w function as vowels; consequently some diphthongs are a combination of a vowel with y, or a combination of a vowel with w. Knowledge of diphthongs is evaluated here.

A. Define the term diphthong:

B. In the words listed randomly below, find the six words that contain a diphthong. In each of these six words, underline the two letters that make up the diphthong.

| | | |
|---|---|---|
| oil | float | built |
| see | owl | few |
| bowl | they | couch |
| boy | pour | each |

| Answer Key |
|---|

**Vowels: Long and Short**

A. Long vowel sounds                                                         Long

| | | | |
|---|---|---|---|
| 1. all | ask | *apron* | (a) |
| 2. *eager* | early | edge | (e) |
| 3. ignore | *idle* | irrigate | (i) |
| 4. odd | *ocean* | order | (o) |
| 5. up | urge | *use* | (u) |

B. Short vowel sounds                                                     Short

| | | | |
|---|---|---|---|
| 1. ace | all | *at* | (a) |
| 2. eagle | earn | *engine* | (e) |
| 3. ice | *ill* | irk | (i) |
| 4. *octave* | owl | over | (o) |
| 5. *ugly* | use | urgent | (u) |

**Vowel Generalizations**

A. If *aif* were a syllable in a word:

1. The *a* would probably sound like the *a* in *ate*.

2. The *i* would be silent.

3. When there are two vowels (in this case, *a* and *i*) in a syllable, the first is usually long and the second is silent, as in *aid* and *note*.

B. If *ek* were a syllable in a word:

1. The *e* would probably sound like the *e* in *end*.

2. When there is one vowel (here, *e*) followed by a consonant in the same syllable, that vowel is usually short, as in *at* and *up*.

C. If *bu* were a syllable in a word:

1. The *u* would probably sound like the *u* in *use*.

2. When there is one vowel (here, *u*) in a syllable, but it is at the end of the syllable, it is usually long, as in *be* and *clover*.

Excerpted by permission of the publisher from Durkin, D., *Phonics Test for Teachers*, (New York: Teachers College Press, ©1964 by Teachers College, Columbia University. All rights reserved.).

*(continued)*

## Digraphs

A. A consonant digraph is a combination of two consonants representing a sound unlike that of either of the individual consonants.

B.     1 <u>th</u>ief          stain          2 cou<u>gh</u>          dumb
       3 <u>ch</u>alet        4 <u>ph</u>ase        5 fi<u>sh</u>            write
          crust            skip             try           6 <u>th</u>ere
       7 sti<u>ng</u>         plane          8 ri<u>ch</u>           brown

## Consonant Blends

A. Consonant blends combine the regular sounds that each single letter represents in a letter team.

B.     <u>bl</u>ank          comb           shout          <u>tr</u>ap
       kite             <u>spr</u>ing          <u>tw</u>ig           camel
       <u>gr</u>ain          ga<u>sp</u>           foam           gnaw
       <u>spl</u>it          write            cane           ru<u>sty</u>

## Diphthongs

A. A diphthong is a combination of two vowels recording a sound unlike that of either vowel. (Here, *y* and *w* function as vowels.)*

   *Technically, too, a diphthong is a kind of sound which, in the process of being made, requires a change in the mouth position. It is for this reason that vowel combinations like *au* (auto) and *oo* (look) are not diphthongs.

   Also to be remembered is that a diphthong is a particular sound, not just a particular combination of letters. This is why *ou* is considered a diphthong in *couch* but not in *four*.

B. Before checking your answers, write the diphthongs (underlined in the words below) in the parentheses before the numbers in the Summary space of the test booklet. List the diphthongs in the order in which they are numbered here. Then check the appropriate Right or Wrong blank for each diphthong.

       1. <u>oi</u>l           float           built
          see          2 <u>ow</u>l           3 f<u>ew</u>
          bowl         4 th<u>ey</u>           5 c<u>ou</u>ch
       6 b<u>oy</u>            pour            each

# References

Adams, M. (1990). *Beginning to read: Thinking and learning about text.* Cambridge, MA: Harvard University Press.

Ayers, L.R. (1993). *The efficacy of three training conditions on phonological awareness of kindergarten children and the longitudinal effect of each on later reading acquisition.* Unpublished doctoral dissertation, Oakland University, Rochester, MI.

Bear, D.R., Invernizzi, M., Templeton, S., & Johnston, F. (1996). *Words their way.* Saddle River, NJ: Prentice Hall.

Berliner, D., & Biddle, J. (1995). *The manufactured crisis.* Reading, MA: Addison–Wesley.

Bond, G., & Dykstra, R. (1967). The cooperative research program in first–grade–reading instruction. *Reading Research Quarterly, 2,* 1–142.

Bond, G., & Dykstra, R. (1997). The cooperative research program in first–grade instruction. *Reading Research Quarterly, 32,* 345–427.

Chall, J. (1967). *Learning to read: The great debate.* New York: McGraw–Hill.

Chall, J. (1983). *Learning to read: The great debate* (Updated ed.). New York: McGraw–Hill.

Clay, M.M. (1989) *The early detection of reading difficulties.* Portsmouth, NH: Heinemann.

Clay, M. (1991). *Becoming literate: The construction of inner control.* Portsmouth, NH: Heinemann.

Clymer, T. (1963/1996). The utility of phonic generalizations in the primary grades. *The Reading Teacher, 50,* 182–187.

Cunningham, P., & Cunningham, J. (1992). Making words: Enhancing the invented spelling–decoding connection. *The Reading Teacher, 46,* 106–114.

Downing, J. (1979). *Reading and reasoning.* New York: Springer–Verlag.

Durkin, D. (1964). *Phonics test for teachers.* New York: Teachers College Press.

Flesch, R. (1955). *Why Johnny can't read.* New York: Harper.

Fox, B.J. (1996). *Strategies for word identification.* Columbus, OH: Merrill.

Galda, L., Cullinan, B., & Strickland, D. (1997). *Language, literacy, and the child.* Orlando, FL: Harcourt Brace.

Gaskins, I., Ehri, L., Cress, C., O'Hara, C., & Donnelly, K. (1996–1997). Procedures for word learning: Making discoveries about words. *The Reading Teacher, 50,* 312–327.

Goodman, K.S. (1993). *Phonics phacts.* Portsmouth, NH: Heinemann.

Goswami, U., & Bryant, P. (1990). *Phonological skills and learning to read.* Hillsdale, NJ: Erlbaum.

Graves, D. (1983). *Writing: Teachers and children at work.* Portsmouth, NH: Heinemann.

Heilman, A. (1989). *Phonics in proper perspective* (6th ed.). Englewood Cliffs, NJ: Merrill/Prentice Hall.

Juel, C. (1993). Teaching phonics in the context of the integrated language arts. In L. Morrow, J. Smith, & L. Wilkinson (Eds.), *Integrated language arts: Controversy to consensus* (pp. 131–154). Boston, MA: Allyn & Bacon.

Juel, C., Griffith, P., & Gough, P. (1986). Acquisition of literacy: A longitudinal study of children in first and second grade. *Journal of Educational Psychology, 78,* 243–255.

Kibby, M. (1983). What reading teachers should know about reading proficiency in the U.S. *Journal of Reading, 37,* 28–40.

Korkeamaki, R., & Dreher, M.J. (1993). Finland, phonics, and whole language: Beginning reading in a regular sound–letter correspondence language. *Language Arts, 70,* 475–482.

Krashen, S.D. (1993). *The power of reading: Insights from the research.* Englewood, CO: Libraries Unlimited.

Lapp, D., & Flood, J. (1978). *Teaching reading to every child.* New York: Macmillan.

Moustafa, M. (1995). Children's productive phonological recoding. *Reading Research Quarterly, 30*(3), 464–476.

Moustafa, M. (1997). Reconceptualizing phonics instruction. In C. Weaver (Ed.), *Reconsidering a balanced approach to reading* (pp. 135–157). Urbana, IL: National Council of Teachers of English.

National Commission on Excellence in Education. (1983). *A nation at risk: The imperative for educational reform.* Washington, DC: U.S. Department of Education.

Perfetti, C., Beck, I., Bell, L., & Hughes, C. (1987). Phonemic knowledge and learning to read are reciprocal: A longitudinal study of first grade children. *Merrill-Palmer Quarterly, 33,* 283–319.

Powell, D., & Hornsby, D. (1993). *Learning phonics and spelling*. New York: Scholastic.

Pressley, M. (1994). More about whole language methods of reading instruction for students at risk for early reading failure. *Learning Disabilities Research & Practice, 9*, 157–168.

Read, C. (1971). Pre-school children's knowledge of English phonology. *Harvard Educational Review, 41*, 1–34.

Read, C. (1975). *Children's categorization of speech sounds in English* (Research Report No. 17). Urbana, IL: National Council of Teachers of English.

Rutherford, W. (1968). Learning to read: A critique. *The Elementary School Journal, 69*, 72–83.

Snow, C., & Tabors, P. (1996). Intergenerational transfers of literacy. In *Family literacy: Directions in research and implications for practice* (pp. 73–80). Washington, DC: U.S. Department of Education, Office of Educational Research and Improvement.

Stahl, S.A. (1992). Saying the "p" word: Nine guidelines for exemplary phonics instruction. *The Reading Teacher, 45*, 618–625.

Stanovich, K. (1994). Romance and reality. *The Reading Teacher, 47*, 280–291.

Strickland, D. (1994–1995). Reinventing our literacy programs: Books, basics, balance. *The Reading Teacher, 48*, 294–302.

Treiman, R. (1985). Onsets and rimes as units of spoken syllables: Evidence from children. *Journal of Experimental Child Psychology, 39*, 161–181.

Vahapassi, A. (1977a). *On the structure and variability of reading skill in Grade 3 of the comprehensive school in school year 1973–1974* (Report No. 283). Jyvaskyla, Finland: University of Jyvaskyla, Institute for Educational Research.

Vahapassi, A. (1977b). *The level of reading and writing in Grade 6 of the comprehensive school in school year 1974–1975* (Report No. 88). Jyvaskyla, Finland: University of Jyvaskyla, Institute for Educational Research.

Vahapassi, A. (1987). *The level of reading comprehension in the Finnish comprehensive school: Publication series A* (Research Report No. 10). Jyvaskyla, Finland: University of Jyvaskyla, Institute for Educational Research.

Venezky, R. (1973). Letter sound generalizations of first-, second-, and third-grade Finnish children. *Journal of Educational Psychology, 64*, 288–292.

Weaver, C. (1994). *Reading process and practice.* Portsmouth, NH: Heinemann.

Weaver, C. (1997). Experimental research: On phonemic awareness and on whole language. In C. Weaver (Ed.), *Reconsidering a balanced approach to reading* (pp. 321–371). Urbana, IL: National Council of Teachers of English.

Wylie, R., & Durrell, D. (1970). Teaching vowels through phonograms. *Elementary English, 47,* 787–791.

Yopp, H. (1992). Developing phonemic awareness in young children. *The Reading Teacher, 45,* 696–703.

Yuill, N., & Oakhill, J. (1991). *Children's problems in text comprehension.* New York: Cambridge University Press

# Index

*Note*: Page references followed by *f* indicate figures.

## A

ACTIVITIES: home, 87–89; homework, 87
ADAMS, M., 7, 48, 96
ADVANCED BEGINNING READERS, 86–87
ALPHABET: strategies that support learning, 56–58
ANALOGIES: onset–rime, 63–66
ANALYSIS, STRUCTURAL, 7, 16*f*, 17
ANALYTIC PHONICS, 31
ANECDOTAL RECORDS, 74, 77*f*
APPLICATION, 34, 37
ASSESSMENT, 35, 37; commercially prepared tools for, 44–45; emerging literacy, 74, 75*f*; informal classroom, 43–47; standardized tests, 44–45; teacher-prepared, ongoing strategies, 46–47
AUDITORY DISCRIMINATION, 34
AYERS, L.R., 6, 96

## B

BACKGROUND KNOWLEDGE, 16*f*, 17
BASAL READERS, 33*f*, 33–34
BEAR, D.R., 62, 96
BECK, I., 6, 97
BEGINNING LITERACY PROGRAMS, 85–87
BEGINNING READERS, 28–30; advanced, 86–87; strategies that support, 53–66; text that can be used with, 35, 36*f*
BEGINNING WRITERS, 28–30; spelling strategies used by, 19, 21*f*; strategies that support, 53–66
BELL, L., 6, 97
BERLINER, D., 11, 96
BIDDLE, J., 11, 96
BOND, G., 10, 96
BOOKS: library, 30–39; trade, 30–39. *See also* Texts
BRYANT, P., 18, 97

## C

CAREGIVERS. *See* Parents
CHALL, J., 10, 48, 96
CHECKLISTS, 74, 75*f*, 76*f*–77*f*

CLASSROOM ASSESSMENT, 43–47
CLAY, M., 46, 75f, 96
CLYMER, T., 39, 96
CODE–DRIVEN PHONICS, 48–52
CODING: DECODING, 15, 16f, 67–71; encoding, 15
COMMERCIALLY PREPARED ASSESSMENT TOOLS, 44–45
COMMUNITY: articulating phonics program to, 81–89
CONFIGURATION CUES, 16f, 16–17
CONSONANT BLENDS, 93
CONSTRUCTIVE SPELLING, 20. *See also* Invented spelling
COOPERATIVE RESEARCH PROGRAM IN FIRST GRADE READING INSTRUCTION ("FIRST–GRADE STUDIES") (BOND & DYKSTRA), 10
COPYING, 27
CRESS, C., 18, 97
CROSS CHECKING, 17
CUES, 15; configuration, 16f, 16–17; environmental, 15, 16f; graphophonic, 16f, 17; picture, 16, 16f; semantic, 14, 16f, 17; structural analysis, 16f, 17; syntactic, 14, 16f, 17; three systems of, 17
CULLINAN, B.E., 45f, 97
CUNNINGHAM, J., 61, 96
CUNNINGHAM, P., 61, 96
CURRICULUM: frameworks for decoding instruction, 67–71, 68f–69f, 70f–71f, 72f–73f; shaping, 67–80
CURRICULUM GOALS, 86

**D**
DECODING, 15, 16f
DECODING INSTRUCTION: curriculum frameworks for, 67–71
DEVELOPMENTAL SPELLING, 20. *See also* Invented spelling
"DICK AND JANE" READERS, 9
DIFFERENTIATED INSTRUCTION, 86
DIGRAPHS, 92, 95
DIPHTHONGS, 93, 95
DISCRIMINATION: auditory, 34; visual, 34
DONNELLY, K., 18, 97
DOWNING, J., 50, 96
DREHER, M.J., 51, 97
DURKIN, D., 96, 90
DURRELL, D., 63, 99
DYKSTRA, R., 10, 96

**E**
"ECLECTIC" APPROACHES, 52; *McGuffey Eclectic Readers*, 8

Ehri, L., 18, 97
EMERGENT SPELLERS, 22f
EMERGING LITERACY DEVELOPMENT: assessing, 74, 75f
ENCODING, 15
ENVIRONMENTAL CUES, 15, 16f
EXTENSION, 34–35

## F

FINLAND, 50
FIRST GRADE: Cooperative Research Program in First Grade Reading Instruction ("First-Grade Studies") (Bond & Dykstra), 10; curriculum framework for, 69–70, 70f–71f; handwriting, 27, 28f; work samples, 74–78, 78f; writing, 28–29, 29f
FLESCH, R., 9, 96
FLOOD, J., 9, 97
FOWLER, D., 1–2
FOX, B.J., 17, 96

## G

GALDA, L., 45f, 97
GASKINS, I., 18, 65, 97
GENERALIZATIONS: vowel, 40, 91–92, 94
GOODMAN, K.S., 41, 97
GOSWAMI, U., 18, 97
GOUGH, P., 5, 97
GRADE 1. *See* First grade
GRADE 2. *See* Second grade
GRAMMAR, 14, 16f
GRAPHOPHONIC CUES, 16f, 17
GRAVES, D., 26, 97
GRIFFITH, P., 5, 97
GROUPING: whole-group instructional format, 41
GUIDED READING/WRITING, 43f

## H

HANDWRITING, 27, 28f
HEILMAN, A., 97
HOLISTIC APPROACHES, 48–52
HOME ACTIVITIES, 87–89; Read-At-Home Log, 79f, 80; Reading-At-Home form, 79f, 80
HOME AND SCHOOL CONNECTIONS, 87
HORNSBY, D., 21, 22f–24f, 92

HUGHES, C., 6, 97

## I

*I Went Walking* (WILLIAMS), 35, 36f, 37
INDEPENDENT READING: monitoring, 80
INDEPENDENT SPELLERS, 24f
INFORMAL CLASSROOM ASSESSMENT, 44–47
INSTRUCTION: comprehensive and balanced programs, 51–52; decoding, 67–71; differentiated, 86; language arts, 41–42; literacy, 6f, 26–47, 85–86; phonics, 28–29, 82–83; in sound–letter relationships, 81–82; whole–group format, 41; for word identification, 6f. *See also* Teaching
INSTRUCTIONAL MATERIALS, 30–39
INTEGRATED LANGUAGE ARTS PROGRAMS, 12, 39–42
INVENTED SPELLING, 20, 84, 85; EXAMPLE, 19, 20f
INVERNIZZI, M., 62, 96

## J

JOHNSTON, F., 62, 96
JUEL, C., 5, 61, 97

## K

KIBBY, M., 11, 97
KINDERGARTEN: curriculum framework for, 67–70, 68f–69f; invented spelling, 19, 20f; *Miss Bindergarten Gets Ready for Kindergarten* (Slate), 55–56
KNOWLEDGE: background, 16f, 17; of narrative structure, 55; sound–letter, 21f; of word recognition, 74, 76f–77f; of words and word parts, 21f
KORKEAMAKI, R., 51, 97
KRASHEN, S.D., 50, 97

## L

LANGUAGE: Finnish, 50; of literacy, 36–37
LANGUAGE ARTS: integrated programs, 12, 39–42; teaching, 40–41
LANGUAGE ARTS INSTRUCTION, 41–42; whole–to–part–to–whole framework, 42, 43f. *See also* Instruction
LANGUAGE PATTERNS: extending, 56
LAPP, D., 9, 97
LEARNING THE ALPHABET, 56–58
LEARNING PHONICS, 53–66; guidelines for, 25f
*LEARNING TO READ: THE GREAT DEBATE* (CHALL), 10
LETTER RECOGNITION, 34
LETTERS: sound–letter knowledge, 21f; sound–letter relationships, 81–82

LIBRARY BOOKS, 30–39
LIBRARY FACILITIES, 86
LITERACY, 6*f*; assessing, 74, 75*f*; language of, 36–37; skills of, 10; as source of enjoyment, 55–56
LITERACY INSTRUCTION, 6*f*, 85–86; changes in, 26–47
LITERACY PROGRAMS, 85–87; total literacy programs, 12
LITERATURE–BASED PROGRAMS, 38
LOOK–AND–SAY METHOD, 8

## M

MANN, H., 8
*McGUFFEY ECLECTIC READERS*, 8
MEANING, 14, blending skills with, 42, 43*f*
MEANING–DRIVEN APPROACHES, 48–52
MEMORY: visual, 21*f*
*MISS BINDERGARTEN GETS READY FOR KINDERGARTEN* (SLATE), 55–56
MODELING, 36
MONITORING AT–HOME AND INDEPENDENT READING, 80
MONITORING PROGRESS, 72–80, 87
MORPHEMES, 19
MOUSTAFA, M., 18, 97

## N

NARRATIVE STRUCTURE: knowledge of, 55
*A NATION AT RISK* (NATIONAL COMMISSION ON EXCELLENCE IN EDUCATION), 11
NATIONAL COMMISSION ON EXCELLENCE IN EDUCATION, 11, 97
NOTES: anecdotal, 74, 77*f*
NOVICE SPELLERS, 23*f*

## O

OAKHILL, J., 44, 99
O'HARA, C., 18, 97
ONSET–RIME ANALOGIES: strategies that support, 63–66
ONSETS, 18

## P

PARENTS: articulating phonics program to, 81–89
PATTERNED TEXTS, 35–39
PERFETTI, C., 6, 97
PHONEMIC AWARENESS, 5–6; strategies that support, 58–59
PHONICS, 4–13, 6*f*, 36, 81–82, 83–84; analytic, 31; articulating to parents, 81–89; best use of, 21–25; code-driven, 48–52; controversy, 4, 5*f*, 8–

13; definition of, 5–7; guidelines for learning and teaching, 25, 25f; holistic approaches, 48–52; how readers and writers use, 14–25; and instructional materials, 30–32; learning, 53–66; reading–based, 50; and spelling, 18–25; synthetic, 31, 50; teaching of, 81; writing–based, 50

PHONICS CUES, 16f

"PHONICS FIRST" APPROACH, 38

PHONICS INSTRUCTION, 28–29, 82–83

PHONICS METHOD, 7

PHONICS QUIZ FOR TEACHERS, 90–95

PHONICS WORKSHEETS, 44–45, 45f

PHONICS–BASED SPELLING, 20. *See also* Invented spelling

PHONOGRAMS, 17

PHONOLOGICAL AWARENESS. *See* Phonemic awareness

PICTURE CUES, 16, 16f

POWELL, D., 21, 22f–24f, 97

PRESSLEY, M., 64, 98

PRINT: functions of, 55

PRINT AWARENESS, 53–54

PRINT CONCEPTS, 54–55

## R

READ, C., 19, 98

READ–AT–HOME LOG, 79f, 80

READERS (STUDENTS): advanced beginning, 86–87; beginning, 28–30, 35, 36f, 53–66; how they use phonics, 14–25

READERS (TEXTS): basal, 33f, 33–34; "Dick and Jane," 9; *McGuffey Eclectic Readers*, 8

READING, 15, 43f; at-home, 79f, 80; guided reading/writing, 43f; independent, 80; repeated readings and response, 36; shared reading/ writing, 43f; strategies for developing foundations of, 53–56; three cueing systems of, 17; word identification strategies for, 15–18, 16f; writing and, 26–30

READING ALOUD: whole reading/writing aloud, 43f

READING–AT–HOME FORM, 79f, 80

READING ERRORS, 46f, 46–47

READING PROBLEMS, 82–83

READING–BASED PHONICS, 50

RECOGNITION: letter, 34; word, 74, 76f–77f

REPEATED READINGS AND RESPONSE, 36

REREADING: whole, 43f

RIMES, 18

RUTHERFORD, W., 10, 98

# S

SECOND GRADE: curriculum framework for, 67–70, 72f–73f

SELF–IMPROVEMENT, 10

SEMANTIC CUES, 14, 16f, 17

SHARED READING/WRITING, 43f

SIGHT WORDS, 31, 33

SKILLS: blending with meaning, 42, 43f; of literacy, 10

SLATE, J., 55

SNOW, C., 56, 98

SOUND–LETTER KNOWLEDGE, 21f

SOUND–LETTER RELATIONSHIPS: instruction in, 81–82

SPELLERS: emergent, 22f; independent, 24f; novice, 23f

SPELLING, 18–25, 84–85; constructive, 20; development of, 21, 22f–24f; developmental, 20; invented, 19, 20, 20f, 84, 85; phonics-based, 20; strategies used by beginning writers, 19, 21f; temporary, 20

SPELLING PATTERNS, 17

STAHL, S.A., 38, 92

STANDARDIZED TESTS, 44–45. *See also* Assessment

STANOVICH, K., 31, 98

STRICKLAND, D.S., 45f, 97, 98

STRUCTURAL ANALYSIS, 7, 16f, 17

SUPPORT PROGRAMS, 86

SYNTACTIC CUES, 14, 16f, 17

SYNTHETIC PHONICS, 31, 50

# T

TABORS, P., 56, 98

TEACHERS: ongoing assessment strategies, 46–47; phonics quiz for, 90–95

TEACHING: language arts, 40–41; phonics, 25, 25f, 81. *See also* Instruction

TEMPLETON, S., 62, 96

TEMPORARY SPELLING, 20. *See also* Invented spelling

TESTS: standardized, 44–45. *See also* Assessment

TEXTS: basal readers, 33f, 33–34; "Dick and Jane" readers, 9; *McGuffey Eclectic Readers*, 8; patterned, 35–39; that can be used with beginning readers, 35, 36f. *See also* Books

TEXTUAL FEATURES, 36

TOTAL LITERACY PROGRAMS, 12

TRADE BOOKS, 30–39

TREIMAN, R., 18, 98

# V

VAHAPASSI, A., 51, 98

VENEZKY, R., 50, 51, 98
VISUAL DISCRIMINATION, 34
VISUAL MEMORY, 21*f*
VOCABULARY: extending, 56
VOWEL GENERALIZATIONS, 40, 91–92, 94
VOWELS: long and short, 91, 94

## W

WEAVER, C., 6, 50, 99
WHOLE READING/WRITING ALOUD, 43*f*
WHOLE REREADING, 43*f*
WHOLE–GROUP INSTRUCTIONAL FORMAT, 41
WHOLE–TO–PART–TO–WHOLE FRAMEWORK, 38, 42, 43*f*
WHOLE–WORD METHOD, 31
*WHY JOHNNY CAN'T READ* (FLESCH), 9
WILLIAMS, S., 35, 36*f*, 37
WORD FAMILIES, 17
WORD IDENTIFICATION: instruction for, 6*f*; strategies for, 15–18, 16*f*
WORD PARTS: knowledge of, 21*f*
WORD RECOGNITION: assessing, 74, 76*f*–77*f*
WORDS: knowledge of, 21*f*; sight, 31, 33
WORK SAMPLES, 74–78, 78*f*
WORKSHEETS, 44–45, 45*f*
WRITERS: beginning, 19, 21*f*, 28–30, 53–66; how they use phonics, 14–25
WRITING, 15, 27, 43*f*; first grade, 28–29, 29*f*; guided reading/writing, 43*f*; personal attempts at, 28–30; and reading, 26–30; shared reading/writing, 43*f*; strategies for developing foundations of, 53–56; whole reading/writing aloud, 43*f*
WRITING–BASED PHONICS, 50
WYLIE, R., 63, 99

## Y

YOPP, H., 5, 99
YUILL, N., 44, 99